BELIEVEMENT

*Breaking through the
Belief Barrier*

MARK A. CORNELIUS

Quantum
Discovery

A LITERARY AGENCY

ISBN
978-1-961601-23-9 (Paperback)
978-1-961601-24-6 (eBook)

Also included as a bonus in this edition…

The *Believement* Companion

A Study Guide for Breaking Though the Belief Barrier

TABLE OF CONTENTS

ACKNOWLEDGMENTS

Thanks to the following for their contributions and their support in editing the book. You helped me believe!

Patti Cornelius
Shay Cavender
Joe Schrott
Chris Slonecker
Stan Toler
Wendy Witherow

Special thanks to my family and friends during my writing time. I know I've been consumed with this project, and yet you've continued to love me. Consider yourselves all loved back.

Finally, thank You, God, for all that You've done with me. Let this work be about Your purpose.

Believement (verb)— 1. "The act or process of searching for supporting evidence in order to justify one's

belief system. 2. Leading a lifestyle of belief. (noun) 1. A lifestyle reflecting a person's belief.

Origin: 2007 Mark A. Cornelius, Believe +-ment, *Believement*

FOREWORD

I met Mark Cornelius several years ago while visiting Nashville, Tennessee. At the time our mutual good friend Chris Slonecker and Mark were designing a unique method for connecting pastors and church congregations who were looking for new ministerial relationships. At the time, neither Mark nor I realized that the relationship between God and His people and our passion for writing was what brought us together. Since that day, I've consulted with Mark on his terrific book titled *RUT Management: Discovering Adventure in the Routine of Life* and had the opportunity to interact with him on this book titled *Believement: Breaking Through the Belief Barrier* and *The Believement Companion: A Study Guide for Breaking Through the Belief Barrier* in which he details the differences in thought, spirit, and action between those who have yet to discover God's active presence in the world and those who have broken through the *belief barrier.*

Mark points out in this book that unbelief doesn't end on the crossing over. The struggle continues with the direction of lifestyle focus of the believer versus the unbeliever—*Am I seeking a stronger intimate relationship with God, or do I want to deny his existence/ interaction in my life?*

Mark has written *Believement* as a simple dialogue between two people. It's unique in that no Bible references or third-party interpretations are involved. It is designed to be an honest discussion from both perspectives, allowing the reader to ask their own questions and make conclusions regardless of which side of the barrier they reside.

The Believement Companion is a tool that any believer will appreciate—either confronting their own struggle with unbelief, studying and comparing their *Believement Lifestyle* with other believers, or walking with an unbeliever who is wanting to break through.

I encourage any reader to approach these books with an open mind and open heart. Don't think of either book as evangelistic tools, but rather as mirrors meant to help with an honest and compelling look at whom we are from either side of the barrier—what we look like without God in our lives, and what we become once we break through and live out our *believement.*

—Stan Toler
Bestselling Author
Oklahoma City, Oklahoma

CHAPTER ONE

It is always the simple things that change our lives. And these things never happen when you are looking for them to happen. Life will reveal answers at the pace life wishes to do so. You feel like running, but life is on a stroll. This is how God does things.

From *Blue like Jazz*
Donald Miller
(Modern American Author, 1971-)

Adam: *What a day. I can't wait to have one of those special bagels with the… what in the world is that ambulance doing in front of the bookstore? Poor guy, the paramedics are working hard on him, I.that's weird, do I know him? He looks familiar, but.hard to tell with the oxygen mask on. Damn, that's gross! He's a goner. I've never seen anyone turn that shade of gray. I hope they don't have to open him up right out here on the sidewalk. Isn't that why they make ambulances with doors on the back—so they can actually close the doors? And here I am with a front row seat—I've got to get inside fast!*

Now this is a better smell than out there, that's for sure! Is a bookstore supposed to smell this good in the morning? I am so glad they put the little bakery in here—what a great combination, breakfast and a good magazine. I think I'll— shoot, someone took my favorite window seat—oh well, I'll grab my food and a quick cup of coffee and wait him out. He'll leave soon enough.

Josh: *This kid looks really annoyed, I must have taken his favorite table. I don't think he wants a conversation! That's the last thing he has to worry about.*

Quit staring at me you old creep! What is with him? He looks like he'll be ready for an ambulance soon too. Okay, Okay, not fair, he's probably looking through me at the wall menu. Yeah, that's it. He's hungry and…no, he's looking right at me…fine, let's fix this right now.

"Can I help you or something?"

"Excuse me?"

"I said can I help you? You seem to be a little obsessed with my direction."

"Sorry, no, I was just looking at the ambulance."

"Sure. The ambulance is over your left shoulder, I'm on your right side."

"Okay, you got me there. I was looking at both the ambulance and you. No offense, you just look familiar."

"Never met."

"I'm Josh, I come in here on a re—"

"Oops, my bad, I should have been more clear. Never met. Don't want to."

"*Right, I apologize.*" Wow, kid's got a brick for a heart—must have had someone really pummel him early on—hope he finds a way to let that frustration go someday. Lord, please look after him and open a way for someone to be able to reach him. Strange thing, I've always wanted to be the kind of person who could do that—engage in that kind of sharing, but I've never felt comfortable that way, just never was wired for that, I guess. I hope someone, though, can help that boy, he—

"Exactly what are you doing?"

"What?"

"Yeah, I know, we're not talking, but before we don't talk, I have got to know what that is you're doing—that thing with your hands and that whispering stuff…"

"Oh, got me again. I'm, well, I'm having a conversation, and when I have a conversation, I…I talk a lot with my hands."

"Yeah, but I'm a little confused. Before we started having this nonconversation that we are now having and will soon be ending, we weren't having a nonconversation at all. That means we weren't talking—nada, zip. Which begs the question, who exactly were you talking with?"

"Oh, my God."

"Oh my god.this is me leaving."

"You don't believe in God? Why does that scare you?"

"That doesn't scare me. People who talk to themselves scare me. That would be you scaring me."

"Well, do you believe in God?"

"Not enough proof—wait, that's not good enough. Whatever proof there might be makes whatever god people thought existed...uninteresting. Who cares? There. That should make you evaporate into some spooky green vapor. Poof, go away!"

"Gosh, that's amazing, I'm still here. But before *you* disappear, sit down and, just for a second, take a look at that guy out there on the gurney. Do you think he believes in God?"

"Of course he believes in a god, he's toast. He's going to believe in anything, just in case. Look, nice try, but that's just fear tactics. I'm pretty sick of that approach actually, the church and government and business—all trying to scare people into buying whatever they're selling. I've found people to be pretty good and smart all by themselves and don't need someone else always telling them what to do."

"So government and businesses are unnecessary?"

"No, but they need to be available only when needed."

"And God—He should step in only when we need Him?"

"That's pretty much it. Except that suggests the idea that your god was something controlled by people and therefore was probably a concept designed by people, which means this god of yours was created by us, not the other way around."

"Then if man created God, He only exists in the human mind for human needs."

"That's basically how I see it. As I think that through, I guess that means I don't believe a god ever really existed."

"So you think that guy out there believes in God because he's afraid?"

"Damn straight."

"So if that were you out there, you'd believe in God?"

"Whatever. Sure."

"Suddenly from unbelief to belief—fair enough. That's actually what happened with me, why not you? What would you believe about God?"

"Do you mean what would I believe a god does? What would this god look like? What kind of car would your god drive?"

"Skip the transportation part, go with the rest."

"Look, I was just coming in here to grab some coffee and then mind my own business when you started minding it for me. No offense, but I didn't plan on spending time with some old guy talking church."

"Me neither—other than the 'old guy' reference that is. Tell you what. Stick around. I'll buy you that coffee and…whatever. Spend an hour with me, and if this gets too challenging for you, I won't be offended if you get up and walk off."

"Clever. '**If this gets too challenging for you.blah, blah, blah,**' look, I'll hang—the coffee and a Danish sound great—but don't try to play games with me. If I stay, it's because I choose too, not because you have some kind of mojo wisdom I can't live without. And if I do leave, too bad, it'll be my choice'cause you're boring me."

"Why not? Choice is what this is all about."

CHAPTER TWO

Everyone seems to be searching and yearning for answers whatever they may be. And that ends up being some kind of spiritual or religious belief.

Sally Quinn,
Columnist for the Washington Post
American Author and Journalist 1941-

I'm just not capable. This is not what I'm born to do. But I want to, don't get me wrong, I'm just not good at it.

"You're doing it again."

"Doing what?"

"That. 'Talking to some unseen cosmic force with your hands' thing. Look, thanks for the coffee—sorry it took me so long to come back, but there's a line over there—so can you get to your point now?"

"Sure. You said you had a choice to stay or leave. I know why you'll leave, 'cause you're boring me', but why are you staying?"

"Hello, *coffee!*"

"Coffee's cheap. Come on, why choose to stay?"

"Curious, I guess. I want to see how you're gonna pitch your god to me."

"Oh…well, sorry. I'm not going to pitch anything actually, guess you can go if you want to."

"Wait a minute! After all that big buildup, you're not going to give me your big song and dance about the almighty? I thought you had some great and powerful message to share with me? Now who's copping out?"

"The great and powerful message is really a small and very personal message, and I'm not the one who can best explain it."

"Well, if you're not, then who can?"

"If I tell you that, you won't accept it, because I'm telling you about my personal experience. Until I started looking at God as the solution to problems instead of the creator of problems, none of His characteristics made much sense."

"Right, so your idea is that your god didn't make the mess, but your god cleans it up. All we have to do is call him up? Like a maid service or something? I know where you're going with this—you're suggesting that your god cares. Personally, I think, if there was a god, he would just be watching it all happen."

"Like when you watch TV—almost as entertainment or a diversion?"

"Exactly."

"Then why doesn't He do something?"

"What? I don't follow."

"Why doesn't God fix our stuff? More personally, why doesn't He fix your stuff?"

"Right—if this god of yours actually exists and is so powerful and mighty, why doesn't he wave his wand and make everything right and perfect in the world?"

"Go figure—a God of compassion? Then I suppose His actions would be compassionate and nothing else. God is just love? Like a warm blanket on a cold day—an *if* God who is there only *if* we need Him?"

"The god you religious types seem to support sounds more like a big stick you hold behind your back, claiming it's there for protection, but then if someone does something you don't like, the stick comes out and whacks them. The problem is that you think you're the only one holding a stick, and so you assume your god wants the same thing you do. So when a tsunami hits or there's some crisis in the world, you stand up righteously and say, 'Our god is telling us to behave.'"

"Interesting that you would condemn me as being self-righteous by claiming your own opinion to be righteous. I'm very capable of being not right—selfish. But if I am serious about wanting a right relationship with God, I'd better be serious about understanding that what He's trying to tell me and what He's showing me is right. If I don't do that, then I'd be acting as my own god."

"If I were my own god, at least I'd be dependable."

"Dependable, huh? You take action, or make a decision, then another action, and your life just moves ahead. But maybe your actions impact someone else's life. That looks dangerously like responsibility."

"I'm willing to accept that. I'm pretty responsible."

"No kidding. Ever change your mind? Ever procrastinate? Ever forget to do something that affected somebody else's needs?"

"Sure, haven't you?"

"Too many times—I'm not dependable, and by no means am I consistent. I would suggest you don't depend on my responsibility as you would have others depend on yours."

"What are you doing?"

"I'm standing up from my chair and pushing it away."

"No, you're not. You're standing up, pushing your chair away and tossing napkins from the table into the air."

"That's right, and here's a couple of sugar packs for good measure—hey, they fly pretty far, don't they! I'm actually thinking at this moment about juggling both our coffee cups and your plate too—I used to be pretty good at this, want to see?"

"You've lost it—you're radically nuts. Sit down, man, that's embarrassing!"

"That's right. Who knows what I'm capable of doing next! Wanna guess?"

"I get it. You're saying that your god is the only consistent force in the universe and we humans are capable of unpredictably weird stuff. But it's not just our actions—every day unpredictable things happen."

"Such as?"

"Natural disasters, accidents, famine, death— you name it. Do you want some help picking up those napkins?"

"Yeah, I'd appreciate that, and an answer to these: How do unpredictable things make God inconsistent? Do you believe God isn't actively and methodically involved in what happens in the world?"

"You think your god cared—wasn't just a spectator watching the show when things got started?"

"I think He was and is still the writer and producer, and even steps in as a cast member. He acts consistently, even planning solutions when earthquakes and other stuff happen inconsistently."

"Did he plan for ambulance man? You know what? That's what I was really thinking about a minute ago: How—when you've hit the wall—it's best to have someone with you on the way to the ER. You know, someone who has seen a lot of trauma, knows what can happen, an expert at treatment on hand, in case something goes badly. I'd take that any day over some *if* god who you hope and pray makes it all better."

"What is it that says they aren't one and the same? Why can't God use people as a resource?"

"And what says people don't act as helpers on their own?"

"Humor me for a second. Let's both reach out there and pretend that…you are a god. Imagine the idea of you as an all-powerful and yet interactive god planning to create a world full of people you want to relate to. How would you set this all up?"

"Hold it. I still don't get what purpose there would be in me creating more at all? As a great-looking, highly intelligent and intellectual twenty-four—year-old god,

I've obviously thought this out, and I'm not limited by time or space— my angels—I can have angels, right?"

"You're a god, angels are allowed—anything goes!"

"My angels have already been—what's a good word here—*conceived.* What's the need to do or invent anything more—just to whip up and sustain one measly little species that won't even appreciate the effort and who will end up dissing their creator? Wouldn't I, the creator—if all-powerful as claimed—have anticipated this? If I were a god and could foresee cooking up that future, I wouldn't even light the stove."

"You don't know how glad I am you're not a god. But let's keep you in the role just a little longer. What if you just really want to create something very...different...something new? And like you said, you can peek into the future. Not only that, you can play the whole scenario out and see the end result. Because of the natural tendencies of the beings you're creating, you know they're going to one day screw up and either not care or possibly even deny that you exist."

"Exactly why I wouldn't bother, more important things to think about—I've got to buy some new sneakers."

"But what might cause you to want to bother? To create a civilization like that in the first place, even knowing the outcome?"

"Like I said, I wouldn't."

"Because you're afraid of, or frustrated, with the potential result? Wait a minute, you're a god— you can do anything you want and fix it too! Don't worry about sneakers—make yourself a pair and get to work!"

"I'm a god, I should have gotten it right in the first place, which is why I don't think I am a god, or anyone is a god, or there is a god, because it all started off wrong."

"Really? How do you know that?"

"Look at the world, man! Look at what it's turning into! It's nothing to brag about."

"I'm confused. A minute ago you were talking about how people were basically good, now you're saying the world is a mess?"

"Yeah, whatever, the fact is, no god would have let that happen."

"Why not. How have you figured out who God is or isn't, and what He is or isn't doing with the world?"

"I don't think anyone knows. Look, I've done some study of my own. I lean a whole lot more toward Hinduism or Buddhism—what do they call that— Pantheism?—because they see the world as their resource to improve and they think mankind can grow up someday."

"But Pantheists also point out a spiritual connection and don't really explain its origin or its ultimate form."

"It's all energy, man, we're a part of it, and we affect it. The better we do, the better it gets."

"Yeah, whatever. The fact is, by what you've described, it looks like we're headed the wrong direction. Don't Buddhists and Hindus recognize all of us being part of a greater whole?"

"Sure."

"So by being a part of that—*not always, but only sometimes acting for the greater good*—crowd, you're also at times rejecting the greater good."

"Now you see why I'm not very interested in a commitment to any organized religion. I do the best I can—I guess the rest of the world will just have to do the same."

"And the others—Islamists, Jews, Christians, other religious types?"

"You all fight over what your gods look like and don't try to find out what you have in common. Allah wants everyone to pray to him and follow Mohammed by following five pillars. Yahweh wants everyone to pray to him, and—depending on if you're a Jew or a Christian—he wants you to either obey a set of rules no one can possibly follow, or claim you're a piece of crap and let the boss fix the rules so you don't have to follow the rules."

"I don't disagree. It reminds me of a very old story about a warrior preparing for battle. He encounters the angel of God and asks, 'Is God on our side?' The angel replies, 'God is on neither side, the question is, are you on God's side?'"

"That assumes that this god of yours had somehow explained what his side was—"

"And who He is, what He believes and wants me to do. If I can't figure that out before I take a single step in my life, then there's not much point in taking a step."

"How arrogant that you think you can hear your god."

"I didn't say I could physically hear Him, but let me ask you, would being able to recognize God's spiritual presence in my life be arrogant or utterly humbling?"

"Guess that depends on how you define your god, and to do that, you'd have to want to believe there _____ was one.

"And if there is a god, how would you define your relationship with Him?"

"Well, that's pretty obvious, isn't it? If there was a god, he pretty much would have done his thing, and I pretty much do mine, and that's fine with me."

"Fine with you, is it fine with Him?"

"You Christians believe in a forgiving god, wouldn't he forgive me if I screwed up?"

"You want the God you don't recognize to forgive you? What about everyone else's gods, should they forgive you too?"

"Look, if your god or any god did exist, he wouldn't have been partial to one group."

"Really? Why not?"

"I think he would have looked at people on an individual basis."

"A few minutes ago He was too disinterested in human events to do that."

"I'm talking about when we die."

"Right. So when you die, if there's a God and He suddenly becomes interested in you, what's going to happen?"

"He'd decide then."

"Decide what?"

"If I...wait...nothing—if he was a god, then he'd have just accepted me."

"Why?"

"Because your god was supposed to have been full of love."

"Now who's telling God what He should be? So the god you just defined is perfect. Is He without any fault—holy?"

"I have no idea."

"Come on. You either buy into the whole package or you don't. If God is God, then He would have to be far superior to anything else—because there is one thing God can't do. God can't be anything other than God. That's one of the definitions of *holy*: perfect in everything. Anything less is...human."

"Okay, sure."

"Are you?"

"Am I what?"

"Perfect, without fault, holy? For that matter, am I perfect? What about the lady behind the sales counter. She looks pretty well behaved—"

"No—"

"and *Ambulance Guy*—this is his last chance— what about him?"

"I don't know."

"You don't know? That might be pretty important to know if you're about to kick the bucket, don't you think?"

"Nobody's perfect."

"But this *if* God that you think might exist, He's perfect? He's holy? How would something or someone that is perfect and holy be able to coexist with something, someone that isn't? Wouldn't God get His hands dirty hanging around imperfect things? Wouldn't He risk becoming unholy?"

"Well, if there was a god, he'd have figured that out, wouldn't he?"

"I believe so. Both from the perspective of what God wants and from what I want. That way, I don't get the two mixed up—is that what you're suggesting?"

"Yeah, but who's going to define that life, that *pur- pose*—what I want versus the wants of a god? If you define the purpose, then you're just like me—your own god!"

"So God would have to somehow explain His wishes to me, but how?"

"Guess he would have had to make it real easy for you to see or hear what he is and what he wants."

"Guess that means He'd have to create a language—documenting all His wishes."

"Yeah, that would be a way."

"The trick would be not changing His words into my words, seems that would be a real tempting opportunity to grab some power."

"But why, if this god was so great, would you want to do that, change any of his stuff?"

"Maybe I don't choose to admit He's great, because what He wants me to do is hard—doesn't make sense or seems not to help me or others. It might even look dangerous and sometimes inconvenient.

Maybe I don't even want to admit He exists. Maybe I want to do things my way and be left alone."

"Fine, I get your point, but maybe, just maybe, I come up with a way to do what I want and help this god out too?"

"Wow—the implications of that! So if I dare to have a discussion with God about the potential of my godliness—my ability to outthink and outperform Him—what could possibly be the end result? You're suggesting that I can make God into what I want Him to be?"

"Let's go with the assumption that stuff happens to everyone and that this god of yours was uninterested in helping out."

"Okay, you have a low expectation of what God does for you, but what do you think He expects of you?"

"I don't know—maybe just to be nice to other people and not to steal or kill. Junk like that."

"Be a good Boy Scout?"

"Yeah, that's it."

"But you don't see Him doing anything. Why should you worry about doing anything?"

"I have to take on a lot of personal responsibility, to interpret what I think might be in my and others' best interests. That's all."

"I fell into that trap too, wanting to think I was personally reliable, wanting others to see me as a fixer. Sometimes, I even got lucky and did some pretty impressive stuff. That gave me a great sense of power. But it also weighed me down like a load of bricks strapped to my shoulders. I didn't want to blow my next chance at making a good impression, so I avoided hard choices and started looking for selfish solutions—easy choices that didn't fix anything but made me look good. Doing that prolonged potential problems—took the monkey off my back. 'Let someone else fix it later,' I'd say. 'After all, there's only so much time in a day, only so much I can do.'"

"Life can be dicey, too many lawyers, too much liability. Safe is good. The unknown? I like adventure as long as the roller coaster's been tested, but the real unknown with absolutely no foreseen consequences— who wants that?"

"So we just make-believe we're adventurers. Putting on the persona of strength—posers trying to impress...who? Trying to assure...

who—each other? That kind of *fantasy thinking* doesn't work out in the long run."

"Easy fix to that too. Don't depend on one person or one religion. That's the problem. We should be listening to everyone who is working for good solutions."

"Mmmm, that's like bundling up all those religious types you mentioned into one big fluffy, happy family, only you'd also include all of the naturalists and the humanists too?"

"The best of all worlds."

"And the best of all wars: Muslims, Jews, Christians, Buddhists, Socialists, and Humanists— all claiming they hear a 'bigger voice' and insisting everyone follow along."

"Wait, that's my argument, not yours! I have no idea why you think Christians are so great. You said yourself, your kind has started as many wars and grabbed as much power as any group on earth."

"Strangely, I agree with you. True, Christianity isn't about hiding faults—it's about recognizing them. It's about acknowledging them to ourselves and to…well, to God, even celebrating the admission and seeking solutions together."

"Why would I want to do that? I can handle life without the crutch of a god, and I sure don't need to cry to others about my problems. I think we'd all be better off if we just live and let live, you know, let everyone find their own karma. Let me have my own definition of god—if I even want to believe there was one."

"God exists whether or not I recognize Him."

"Really? What does your god want, and what gives you the right to define that?"

"You're assuming I want the same thing God does."

"Don't you? Don't you want a good place to live and peace on earth and for bad things to go away?"

"Sure I want those things, but nothing gives me the right to define God or what He wants. For discussion sake, help me understand in more detail—what do you think God wants?"

"I think if there was a god, he'd want us all to behave ourselves and get along. I think he'd want us to clean up the planet and feed the poor and to stop trying to be more powerful than everyone else. I think he'd want everyone to be happy and well-off and more active in solving their own problems."

"And that guy on the medical gurney out there should not be choosing to knock on God's door for help because that's the job of the paramedics and because, as you would define Him, God is bigger than such a small problem—a struggle between life and death?"

"It's a big universe, if there was a god, he wouldn't be spending his time running around kick-starting cardiac cases."

"But being holy, why doesn't He jump into the fray and settle the argument once and for all?"

"Like I said, if he ever existed, he'd be busy with other things."

"An all powerful God who can do anything, anytime, be anywhere, any place, who is too busy?"

"I need more coffee."

"Me too, I'll stand in line this time."

CHAPTER THREE

Every religion, theory or system of belief that attempts to explain the world requires faith— believing in something that can't fully be proven. At first glance, you may think an atheist is exempt from this rule, but that's not true. An atheist has faith all right—not in a divine God, but in the belief that God doesn't exist.

Richard Wagner,
from an undetermined interview
German Composer, Conductor
and Author 1813-1883

I can't believe *I'm putting up with this. The old man's nice enough, but I don't have time for theology class. Why are they all alike—so righteous and anxious to prove how inadequate or how un-good people are unless they click the heels of their ruby slippers together and say 'There's no one like Jesus' three times out loud? I hate that happy-clappy church stuff.*

"**What are you thinking about?**"

"Huh? What makes you think I'm thinking about anything?"

"It's that 'repeatedly stirring your black coffee, staring off into space' thing that gives you away."

"Busted! I'm trying to figure out why guys like you think making a choice to believe or not to believe in some god is such a huge deal that has to be jumped on right now, as if the world is going to blow up any second?"

"I'm no expert on the end of the world. I sure don't want to force anyone into a decision they aren't ready to make. I do think each of us is presented with the option of choosing to believe in a higher power, deny that existence/power, or simply ignore its significance. I know that when that opportunity presented itself to me, my reaction was to try to ignore it and pretend it wasn't a priority."

"You think not making that choice kills people or something really bad will happen to them?"

"I think making that choice has to happen before anyone truly experiences life. I know that sounds weird—you look pretty alive to me—it's hard to explain."

"Try me. I'm dying to hear this."

"It sounded stupid to me too, and I don't want it to sound like those who do choose to follow God are somehow superior...they do have something though, which those who choose not to follow can't seem to recognize or make sense of. It's the something of life—the thing that is beyond life as we know it."

"Sorry, I'm not convinced. I think people just say they believe in some higher power or some scientific theory of life because it's trendy, or makes them feel good, or it makes them look good to someone else. Sometimes I think it's just easier to tell you self-righteous types exactly what you want to hear. The question is, what is it you really want to hear? If I say, 'Oh yes, I believe in your god,' that might just make you go away for a while.

"You're pretty damn good at this."

"Oooh, what was that, an expletive coming out of the mouth of the high and mighty, not very Christian- like thoughts."

"Christians aren't perfect examples of life, we're just like everyone else—perfect examples of choice. Like that guy out there. He's a great example. By the way, they're stabilizing him."

"Say again?"

"Stabilizing. They're trying to make sure he'll make it to the hospital—sometimes it's the trip that kills you. They want to make sure he's healthy enough, committed to making the journey."

"I know what stabilizing is. I meant I don't understand why he's such a great example of choice?"

"Because if he hasn't already, he's got one to make right now. It could be his last, so it better be his best."

"You see, that's what I'm talking about. Just because he's all up in knots doesn't mean I have to be. I'm not the one on the gurney, and I don't think I'm anywhere near being on one. I don't feel any rush to run to your almighty."

"We were talking about the guy out there, not you."

"Yeah, but you meant me too. You use fear like a whip, cracking it to get the attention of all us poor little heathen people as if to say, 'Careful, we can use this on you too—better choose carefully and better do it now!' You religious groupies don't need stabilizing, you need institutionalizing."

"So if I just left you alone, you'd be just fine, and there'd be no problems in the world?"

"You got it."

"And you think all people choose to base their lives on that kind of thinking?""

"Not...completely. Look, I try to do good things. I think everyone should try to do good things, but I think history is pretty clear—if left to our own devices, we choose based on a selfish need. Even if I were to run out there and try to save Dying Guy, it would probably be because either I knew him and I didn't want to go to his funeral, or because he owes me money, not because I feel some altruistic tendency to heal the sick."

"You want to feel good, or look good, and in turn, you hope others act good, and we'll all pretend we're good to each other while we discreetly go about trying to make sure our individual shopping bags are filled with our own good stuff?"

"Man, you are one cynical dude!

"Actually, I'm just a realist...like you, which takes us back to what you think an *if* God looks like. You're telling me that, if there is a God, He's too big and powerful to be worried and interested in your little world?"

"That's pretty much it, yeah."

"**Is this *if* God of yours all-powerful and all-knowing?**"

"Sure, yeah."

"**So with all that power and knowledge, *if* God has choices to make too. He can make those choices, do anything—anytime He wants to?**"

"Sure. Whatever."

"**He didn't have to give us free will. It would have made everything a lot simpler, wouldn't it? Maybe, way back when, God knew the nature of the people He was going to create. He chose to put in a backup plan to help them along.**"

"Your picture of a lovey-dovey god just doesn't fly."

"**I don't remember using that term to describe God. But if He's not at least partially compassionate, then that makes God a power broker, and I guess before you and I start laying all the bad stuff that happens in the world at His feet, claiming it to all be His fault, answer me this. Does evil exist?**"

"Badness? Sure, and that suggests, from your argument, that your god had created it."

"**Or maybe He created an environment where good and ev... badness aren't tangible things, but choices.**"

"You're saying that a flood or a hurricane is a choice?"

"**Those things aren't good or evil, they're natural occurrences. How I react to them can result in all kinds of good or hideous results. Distinguishing the difference between good and evil is based on my doubt, not on an absence or lack of my faith.**"

"Say again?"

"**I'm not going to get into the garden of Eden discussion with you, and I don't care if you look at it metaphorically or not, but I am going to ask this: What do you think the problem was with humankind eating the fruit of the tree of the knowledge of good and evil?**"

"Uh... that we were bad because we chose to do what we wanted to do?"

"**That's the standard answer. Another question, metaphorical or otherwise, How many kinds of fruit were there on the tree?**"

"Two.no.one.no clue. I thought we weren't getting into the creation story thing. That is such a fable! I don't even think I've ever bothered to read it. I remember some aunt or someone telling it to me a long time ago. What in the world does that have to do with good and bad?"

"If you want to address this symbolically, fine. The *fruit*—just one kind—I have the choice to do one of two things. Either trust God unconditionally to provide all my needs and all my answers—choosing *not* to choose—an absolute demonstration of faith in Him. Or I do not trust in God, deciding on my own what is good and bad. Choosing to choose, measuring to compare—my absolute rejection of faith in Him."

"Ouch—you're hurting my brain. Let me think about that."

"Exactly my point. You shouldn't have to think, just respond. But you choose thought as a delay tactic instead of pursuing a decision of choice, me too."

"Good and evil exist because I chose them into existence?"

"Good and evil can't exist without one another. Even Pantheism suggests there are choices of direction that must be made. You have a free will, so who chooses, you or God?"

"You're saying that the first act of freedom of choice is deciding I want to comprehend/pursue an understanding of the difference between good and evil—I'm making godlike decisions in place of your god. And by trying to make those decisions, I'm trying to be a god?"

"And having to live with the consequences of that freedom of choice."

"But I've always thought that humanity is basically good, with nutjobs and psychopaths being the exception. Are you saying humanity is basically evil, with goodness being the exception?"

"The question itself is a distraction—it answers itself. Every person is capable of great goodness and great evil, but the fact is evil exists in each of us, and society has proven that it is incapable of getting rid of evil or of curing it by doing great good."

"Now that you mention it, I have a choice based on that same argument. I either believe there are two wills, mine and *if* god's (door number one), or I choose to believe there's only one will—mine, which means I'm on my own. I choose door number two."

"Lonely place—door number two."

"I'll be fine, thanks, you can go now."

"Looks like I have a choice too."

"Whatever."

"I think I'll go for door number three."

"Uh, what's door number three?"

"I choose to be incapable."

"I don't follow."

"You've already admitted there are times when things go wrong, when your world appears to fall apart before your eyes. I'm the same way. My tendency is to become more and more confident in my own abilities until something smacks me in the head and I find out just how incapable I am. So I choose to be incapable, not just at the end of that cycle, but all the time. The realist in me knows that no matter how good I look on my own—doing my own thing at any given time—the end results are always the same."

"That's not realism, it's defeatism. You're saying you've given up!"

"That's bad?"

"Damn straight it's bad! Listen, whether or not you and I choose to believe the same thing spiritually—and I know for a fact that you have to agree with me on this—you are challenging me, you are trying to communicate a point, you are sitting here trying to convince me on the value of your beliefs, you have not given up!"

"I see. Let me make sure I've got this straight. I shouldn't choose to give up, but God should?"

"Hey, I have an idea—walk with me for a minute, Okay?"

"We may lose our seats."

"So we do—live dangerously, take a risk, man! Come on. You see all these rows of books and magazines? There's a huge amount of human knowledge here in this store, and this is just one small shop in the scheme of things."

"History, fiction, science, self-help—look, here's one on *Meditating Your Way to Losing Weight*. I wonder if that falls under spirituality, or health and diet?"

"Whatever. Look, my point is this. Touch these, they're real, they are the thoughts and wisdom of people over a whole lot of time and from many cultures. Aristotle, Socrates, Gandhi, Vonnegut…"

"Moses, Jesus, Paul of Tarsus."

"Fine, them too—but what I'm saying is, they can't all be bad. They wrote these things, and these things have helped us be better. The writings and the way to get help is right here to be touched and read, absorbed—"

"And used?"

"Yeah! When we use them, things work better."

"Like Hitler's *Mein Kamph*?"

"Okay, there are exceptions."

"I love the Bible and believe every word of it is the absolute true and inspired Word of God given to mankind. But wars, power struggles, and family breakups have been caused even by those great words when misinterpreted or acted out incorrectly by the wrong person."

"People read and are influenced by other's great works, but in the end, we all have to make personal and cultural choices. Doesn't it make sense that the more great influences we come in contact with, the more likely our choices will be good?"

"Are you saying humans are good because they strive to improve? That by writing out our visions of goodness, and by not giving up on our pursuits, and by learning from each other, we're advancing?"

"I think we're improving as a species—advancing on our own, yes."

"So what God does, doesn't matter?"

"I don't care what your god has done!"

"But you care about what I've done and do. Why?"

"Because you're better than that! You care, you have heart."

"Do you know why I have a heart? Why I care?"

"It doesn't matter—you just do."

"That's exactly the line drawn between us that needs to be crossed because I believe differently than you, and it speaks to every difference of choice between us. The reason I care is the reason we're different."

"But I care too! Isn't my care good enough for you?"

"The fact that you're asking me says that you look at where your care is going to, without any understanding of where it's coming from."

"If it helps people and does good, who cares?

"Define 'good.'"

"Helping, not hurting, opposite of bad."

"Interesting. Where did that definition come from?"

"*Webster*, or whoever the hell makes up words—I don't know!"

"**But you did just make a great point. Some man or woman or group came up with that?**"

"Sure. So?"

"**What if we have the definition wrong? What if there's more to it than just trying to help a lot?**"

"I'm sorry, now my 'good' isn't good enough?

"**That wouldn't be a good thing, would it? I sure want to know that when I go to the effort of mak-**

ing an effort, it's not thrown back in my face with a 'Thanks for playing, but your effort wasn't enough, come back again soon and try harder.' If I kept getting that answer to my attempts of acting with goodness, pretty soon, I'd start choosing not to try as often."

"Your point?"

"**It's back to the choice of fruit in the garden thing—we first learned by comparing our efforts to others, or to history. There were always worse and better examples. So we then started to act incon- sistently, based on each person's choice of conveni- ence—because it was useless to try to be good all the time—nobody was that good, and we got real tired of trying.**"

"Wait. Looking at it that way, why choose to try at all?"

"**Exactly! And if you look not so very hard, you'll see that there are a lot of people who try halfheartedly, or not at all. Sure, there are people who do try to do the right things most of the time, but it makes you wonder if even they doubt sometimes that the attempt is worth it.**"

"I don't think that way—doubtfully."

"**You don't? Yet just this morning you were ready to write off an old man who invited you to engage him in some good conversation.**"

"That's because I didn't see any value in going through with the...oh."

"**We all think that way. I do. I choose, and my choices—as good as they may seem to me—aren't always up to the standard.**"

"The standard? Whose standard? I live in a world where choices have to be made to survive and to move forward. Are you saying the results— the outcome of my choices—are all worthless?"

"**Work backwards. Is the result of your choices, or the reason you made the choice in the first place, more important?**"

"I'm guessing the reason I made the choice, but you're suggesting I'm always aware of why I made a choice, and frankly, I'm not always that tuned in to myself."

"Me neither. One more good reason not to depend on your own choice-making abilities. Does your family love you?"

"What? Yeah, sure they do."

"And if you chose to ignore advice they've given and do something that risks you being in the wrong place, or doing the wrong thing at the wrong time, is that their fault?"

"You're telling me that I shouldn't live near a flood zone because there's a god who loves me?"

"I'm saying that if you choose to live in a place of risk, you need to understand and be prepared for the consequences related to those choices. Are you?"

"Am I what?"

"Prepared for tragedy based on your choices? Do you understand the good and the badness of the environment you live in? For example, do you make a habit of crossing a busy highway at rush hour?"

"Of course not."

"Because you know it's very dangerous. But I bet you ignore lesser dangers, risking harm to yourself or others, because the choices are more subtle. Yet they still exist. You would blame God for tragedy based on circumstances you were aware of but ignored?"

"I don't see anyone else doing any differently."

"Great point. Just for a second, let's give you your godhood back and look at the beings you've created. Would they obey you because, well, because you've designed them to obey you?"

"Now that's what I'm talking about—having that group hanging around all the time to follow my every command. If I were a god, I'd make sure everyone stayed in line."

"And that they worshiped you."

"I don't know about worship, but a god does deserve respect."

"All the time, even when you're doing things and asking them to do things they don't like?"

"A god is a god, ya gotta trust him."

"If one of those beings you created chose not to respect you, what would you do?"

"Fry'em. If they didn't want to come to the party, I would show'em to the door!"

"So no one would choose to share with you anything deeper than platitudes and obligatory praise because that's all you'd ask of them. Wouldn't that get boring? Wouldn't you eventually want someone to respect you, even love you because they—oh, I don't know—because they want to, not because they're programmed to?"

"I wouldn't take the chance to plan my universe with a wildcard in the deck. I'm a god—I can work

the whole thing through to the end. How would I lead or guide everything toward my desired outcome, not the outcome I fear happening, without forcing my new beings to worship...c.orrec.tion...respec.t me?"

"What if one of your choices as a god was that you wanted something to exist that was unique and very special... valuable and.,.well, even fun for you at times? It would be something you could also share with the rest of your creation, but maybe this new thing would require a high maintenance relationship be established with a species—based on a freedom of choice completely foreign to those who already see and relate directly to you. What if you wanted to create a voluntary relationship, with beings that would only recognize the existence of God as an unseen, physically untouched master?"

"Wouldn't work. The *created* would have to totally trust in the presence of a creator they could not actually see or hear. People don't do that."

"But what if they did? What if they chose to do it freely and willingly? Wouldn't a kind of trust develop—an admiration, even a love between the Creator and the created—that would be unlike, and more powerful than, any other kind of relationship yet conceived?"

"Sounds like a lot of work. Like you said, *high maintenance.*"

"Both for the Creator and the created, but I think the created makes it more work than necessary."

"That's stupid, why make something harder than it has to be?"

CHAPTER FOUR

*A necessary consequent of religious belief is the attaching
ideas of merit to that belief, and of demerit to its absence.*

From *Truth*
Francis Wright
British Reformer, 1795—1852

"See, I told you it was worth the gamble. We got our seats back and still have the front row seat to the emergency room soap opera episode outside."

"That was a little cold."

"Yeah, it was. Sorry. I meant what I said—I really do hope he comes out of this all right. Maybe you can help?"

"How so?"

"Can you prove the existence of your god? If you can, maybe that would help me believe he could help Ambulance Guy?"

"An interesting challenge—almost as much so as you proving to me there is no God."

"Oh, that would be easy. Back to the natural dis- asters—disease, famine. If there was a god, people wouldn't die from that stuff. For that matter, why do people have to die at all if there's a god who wants them so badly?"

"Then life should be one big reward? Could death also be the big punishment? How does the existence of disaster and death explain away God? Remember how I told you I used to measure the possibility of God? By that kind of thinking, good fortune and longevity explain Him right back into existence."

"But that's not proof to me there is a god."

"My trying to prove God does or doesn't exist doesn't prove anything. It's pointless because, before trying to prove, I have to take a position, and so the only thing I prove is my opinion. The real question that I had to start asking myself was, Can I prove the nonexistence of God to God?"

"Oh, oh, they just had to jump-start Ambulance Guy. You know what? That brings up a good issue. I hope he makes it and all that, but say he doesn't and let's say there is a heaven, what's the difference between here and there? If it's so great, why do people fight so hard to stay alive, why not just let it happen and go there?"

I pray he makes it too.

"Good question, but the wrong one. First off, are you sure heaven is his ultimate destination? What other options might there be?"

"Good grief! You're not going to sit there and tell me you're one of those 'believe or you'll burn in hell' types, are you?"

"It doesn't matter what I think right now. I've never been beyond this life, so I have to choose how I believe the afterlife will work and continue to live by that belief—"

"Or unbelief. If I don't believe in an afterlife, it really doesn't matter."

"Maybe not, but you were asking about our guy out there—looks like they got him back, by the way, but what happens to him? You said, when we first started talking, you thought he would believe because he's scared to death."

"Well, yeah!"

"But why would he be afraid? If there's nothing beyond this, what does it matter? Or if he's heaven bound, what does it matter? He's lived a good life, and that's that."

"Maybe he has a family and a life he likes, and he's not ready to give it up."

"Sure, that makes sense, and accounts for the fight to stay alive, but it doesn't explain the natural fear you hear coming from and see in people who are on their deathbed, that uncomfortable look at the unknown ahead. Why do people who are dying struggle with that? And for that matter, why do you and I typically shy away from talking about it unless the reminder is right there in front of us?"

"People don't really believe, they doubt. They doubt their lives and their afterlives because they don't under-

stand the unknown things happening around them and they doubt the future they can't see in front of them."

"But you said before that you don't think that way—doubtfully."

"Yeah, you made your point—we all fall into that trap. But if I'm going to choose to believe there was a god, it's going to be because I *want* to believe there was a god, not because I *have* to."

"Unless you're on your deathbed, then you might believe because you're afraid."

"Just covering the bases."

"I doubt it."

"You doubt what; that people believe in their god out of fear?"

"It was a challenge that was once put to me. Someone asked me if I believed in God. I told them I didn't think there was enough proof that God exists. The other person then said, 'I doubt it.' He knew I didn't understand his response, so he explained, 'I doubt that you don't believe in God.'"

"You're saying that because I doubt a god existed that I believe there was a god?"

"I can't speak for you. I just remember how I used to justify my actions and lifestyle. It went something like this. I perceived the idea of God as a helper/ nonhelper. Most of the time, I didn't see any evidence that He was active, so I rationalized that He didn't exist.

"You thought that way? That doesn't sound like your kind of thinking at all!"

"Oh, it was me all right. Sometimes I wanted or needed real help because of some tragedy or something I wanted badly, so I'd experiment

with a request. If things turned out the way I thought they should, it strengthened my interest in the potential of an actual Supreme Being. If things fouled up, it affirmed what I actually thought deep down, *A real God would be more visible in this world,* and I would dismiss the notion of a Universe Creator."

"I approach the 'god-no-god' question a little differently, more globally. I can pretty much take care of myself—I don't need a crutch. If I need help, there are people and organizations out there for that, but I'm just a small part of this world. If there was a god, I don't see him having fixed the stuff that really needed fixing."

"Like?"

"War, famine, disease, earthquakes—the usual. Some things I think we're responsible for, but some things just…happen. *If* god wouldn't have just planned solutions as you call them, he wouldn't have let those things happen in the first place."

"I used to think like that too, then I started questioning it another way. If there was a God, why wouldn't He allow stuff like that to happen?"

"That's the way you believers think—no matter which religion I read or hear about or whose actions I see! Even now I can hear it when you define your so- called god relationship. If someone in the crowd started handing out money to everyone in this place, it would be because your gods have smiled on you, but if I pull out a gun and start picking off people one by one, it's

because we're not living according to the way you think life should be lived. Then you plaster your gods all over your statements to endorse what you want, and therefore, it makes you right, and everyone is just expected to follow along because your gods told you this was the way to do it."

"Got one?"

"What? Got one what?"

"A gun. I want to make sure I don't tick you off."

"Let me look in my backpack—nope, don't have a gun—come on, you know I'm not the type."

"That's all right, I think I have one in my bag here somewhere, hold on a second while I look—"

"Not funny, you can stop now."

"I'm not being funny at all. What makes you think I was being funny? I think it's just a little too crowded in here. Give me a minute, and once I find the darned thing, I'll fix that."

"Listen, just settle down and let's talk this through!"

"Shhh. Keep your voice down. You'll draw attention, and that might set me off. Talking isn't helping anyways—sometimes you just have to act. Where is that thing? I thought I had it in here somewhere… hey, I think I've found it."

"Are you crazy? I…please, don't do anything that—please!"

"Shoot."

"No, don't shoot!"

"I mean I can't shoot, it's just a flashlight. Now I remember. I don't even own a gun! Will you please sit down? Everybody in the room is staring at you."

"That was not…not amusing!"

"But it was a great example. Ridiculous things do happen. You, me, none of us know what those around us are truly capable of—good or bad, sane or insane."

"You think I'm capable of something like that?"

"It doesn't matter to me if you're capable or not. I know for a fact what would happen to me if you or anyone or any unpredictable event took my life."

"You know for a fact—how can you know for a fact what will happen to you after death?"

"It must be frustrating to not understand people who believe so intently in something that you can't see. What goes through your mind when you can't see what believers appear to believe in and perceive so clearly?"

"You believe so strongly that your god would save you if your life was threatened?"

"I believe that strongly that my God has already saved me, not from you or physical circumstances, but from myself. He fixed me spiritually and, in doing so, showed me how to overcome unbelief, even when faced with unbelievable circumstances in a crazy world."

"Prove it."

"Prove what?"

"That your god was here before us and that the fix, as you call it, isn't just some man-made myth to give false comfort or to control others."

"You're asking me to break the *belief barrier* between us, and I'm incapable of doing that. It's the paradox of faith. I can't prove God's existence if you're not willing to put aside your unbelief for a moment. If you do that, then suddenly, you're willing to believe in God, so His existence becomes immediately evident."

"I have to prove to me that a god has existed?"

"No proof is necessary, only acceptance. The question isn't 'Is there a God?' The question is 'What if there is a God and I choose not to believe in Him— and I'm wrong?'"

"Problem with that is what happens when two or more *religious types* like you claim different ways of belief to be right, when different religions with different gods claim different directions of faith to be the right way?"

"I think people base their spiritual beliefs on foundations just like we do social and political beliefs. That also suggests there are those who are very active in their beliefs and others that may just be along for the ride. Inactive—who don't place much or any value in committing to a belief."

"Sure, that makes sense."

"I'd like to think I fall into the first category, and so it stands to reason that I have to investigate and ultimately take a stand based on my belief."

"Okay."

"Once I make that commitment, it's very hard for me to veer away from my justification of that belief, even in the face of what seems like irrefutable evidence."

"You just nailed your religion to the wall."

"I just nailed anyone who believes passionately in anything to the wall. Here's the problem—something has to be right. Would you agree with that?"

"Some *thing*? You mean some god?"

"I mean there has to be some fundamental element that holds everything together. The universe, and us along with it, had to have some kind of origin. Can you argue that?"

"We could have come from aliens."

"I have no doubt that you may have, but even aliens had to have an origin, right?"

"O…kay…"

"Here's what I'm getting at. I believe what I believe because of a couple of things that may be stumbling blocks for you. They have to do with origins, and it's those origins that may divide us or bring us together."

"Oh, oh, are you aiming at the garden of Eden thing?"

"Before that actually. Can something come from nothing?"

"Nope."

"Then where did *something* come from?"

"Big Bang. Duh!"

"Oh, oh, are you resting your belief or unbelief on evolutionism? That tiny little speck of compressed matter in the center of the universe that somehow decided to explode out one sunny day, where did that come from?"

"No clue."

"I have one. Instead of asking if something can come from nothing, what happens to your reasoning if you ask, can nothing come from something?"

"What? Oh, I see, you're trying to mess with me there, you're suggesting that your god was there to speak matter into existence. Where did your god come from?"

"The *belief barrier* again. Either I choose to believe God has existed before time and space and has never had a beginning and will never have an end or I don't."

"I don't."

"No problem with me. What do you believe?"

"Wait a minute, that's not relevant. There are lots of possibilities."

"But the one I just suggested isn't one of them."

"Right you are!"

"Why not?"

"Because it's improbable *and* impossible."

"Who says?"

"Lots of people do—I do!"

"But what if it were possible? Would that explain away a lot of the differences and doubt that exist between believers?"

"Just claiming something can be doesn't make it so."

"Including the claim that there is no God, and that He's not eternal?"

"Point taken, but it doesn't prove your belief."

"Nope, you'll have to do that."

"You're asking me? I'm not claiming to have a god."

"Really? Which category that we've discussed do you fall into? Are you an active or an inactive participant in belief?"

"Active, I guess."

"Active believers don't guess."

"Active. There, happy?"

"One more time then, and this time give me the active believer answer, Do you believe without a doubt, would you bet your life on it, can you look me straight in the face without any sarcasm whatsoever and say there is no God?"

"No."

"No what?"

"No…I don't know, if there was a god."

"Which, means there could be?"

"Could be."

"And if God 'could be,' He would have to be in existence before all other things. He could *not* have been created by some other force, meaning He was never created, but simply has and will always exist?"

"That's not simple, but it is rational—if a god existed."

"So get off the fence. Either God exists or He doesn't. There is no 'could be' unless you've changed your mind and want to drop back into the inactive category."

"I hate you."

"I don't doubt it. Faith is crucial to any belief. In the end, everything can be unproven—even my own existence."

"Fine, fine. There was a god who created this place. Happy?"

"I wasn't unhappy. What about you, you happy?"

"Before you came along!"

"Understood. You don't want people who do have a god to bother you. You live life ignoring them and also ignoring the question of the existence of God, pretending that everything is all right. But everything isn't all right, is it? Stuff happens, like you've said. And when it happens, you wonder deep down why you are singled out or that if there is a God why He allows stuff to happen that makes you hurt or that messes up your cozy life? And the next logical conclusion is, there is no God or else He wouldn't let stuff happen that hurts me."

"Which is the most confusing part to me. I've caved. I'm willing to accept there was a god, but that doesn't make him the good guy on the white horse riding in to save the day all the time."

"The fact that God is invited in and out of peoples' lives doesn't explain His actions. I still want God to do what I want God to do, but most times, I'm not willing to do what God wants me to do."

"You're willing to tell everyone else how great your god is, but you're unwilling to admit your god's instructions are better than you?"

"Lots of times I'm unwilling to admit I need Him. That's the problem. He was here before me, before anyone, and has the solutions all laid out. Most of the time, I'm just too stubborn and proud to admit I can't handle things on my own."

"There you go again, making my argument for me! Like I said, I'll buy the notion of a god, but Christianity has no claim on him. Know what? I've been to your churches. I saw a lot of people there saying exactly that. 'Oh yes, I see the light now, I believe, praise god, hallelujah!'"

"So?"

"I heard'em saying it. I heard'em singing it, but you know what I saw in their eyes? Know what I saw in their actions as they ushered me out after the service? What I saw was caution, fear, like they were saying the words and doing what they did almost as if to avoid being caught not believing so that they wouldn't have to explain to someone else that they doubted or downright just didn't buy in at all—it looked fake. But it wasn't a fakeness put on for me. It was a fakeness put on for all the other fakers in the crowd."

"And your point?"

"Don't you get it? I don't buy into Christianity because Christianity doesn't buy into itself. You doubt, and you're afraid someone is going to catch you doubting, so you sing louder about your un-doubt. The weird thing is, you aren't so afraid that your god will catch you, isn't that funny? Your doubt tells you deep down that your god may exist but that your god maybe doesn't really care about you as much as you'd like to believe. Actually, you're all afraid that other people around you, who also doubt and are pretending, are going to catch you doubting and pretending."

"Strange, isn't it? If only all of us knew that we are all doubting, we'd probably all become unitarians or agnostics, or some highly intellectual brand of belief—anything but dumb blind Christians! Did it ever occur to you that Christianity is the only faith that people and cultures attack for its followers' lack of faith? Yet every religious person of any faith encounters doubts about the existence of God. If they didn't, why wouldn't there be just one religious choice?"

"You agree that someone can find and define their god in different ways! Look at that—we may actually agree on something. I'm willing to admit that there are lots of unexplained things that go on in the world and that scientific types can't explain it all. What I don't agree with is that any one group has the only answer about whom or what god was. I think Buddhists and Krishna probably have as strong a faith as most Christians ever will, and their god works for them as well or maybe better than your god."

"It doesn't matter if mine or theirs is better because—based on what you just described—I don't believe in God."

"Now you're the atheist? I don't get your argument."

"Let's say for a moment that I'm the guy out there in the ambulance struggling for life. I'm scared to death, and I know this might be my last shot at getting things right. I've never been a religious type, but I want to make sure I don't leave any loose ends behind, and I also want to cover my bases in case there really is an afterlife. Who do I reach out to?"

"Uh, a god?"

"Which god?"

"Any—*all*, it doesn't matter. They're *all* the same."

"Wait a minute. Islam states that I must denounce all other gods and follow the laws of the prophet Mohammed. Buddha says I need to be at one with all life, Judaism says I must love God with all my heart and recognize no other god before the one true God. Christianity says

that no one may come to God except through Jesus Christ. Krishna says…frankly, I don't get Krishna. So who's right?"

"Nobody! Even by asking 'Who is my god?' I fail because the god would have defined himself before… anything. Neither you nor I can define him in terms of our trapped questions—like you said—good versus evil. By trying to, we divide ourselves from the reality of god."

"That's the most profound thing I've heard you say all day. So if one is the wrong interpretation, they're all faulty?"

"Who can be right?"

"How about God? If I had just recently started believing in God, I think I'd want to know beyond a doubt what He was all about—I'd want Him pretty well defined. Come to think of it, I think He'd want me pretty committed to who I am too. After all, I don't want to get all mixed up about who's God and who's not."

"You throwing a little sarcasm at me?"

"Just to make a point. Someone has to be right. If God hasn't explained Himself to us well enough and some group hasn't gotten the message, then He's a pretty lousy communicator, and something tells me that's not the issue."

"Good point. Of course, your claiming that makes you right?"

"Before I respond to that, do you think people who seek God are looking for reasons *to* believe or *not to* believe?"

"You would think because they want to believe."

"And yet when you ask me, or for that matter, when I get into conversations or read, or even pray to God, my first inclination is to argue and dispute rather than listen and consider. Our conversation is a great example. Are you and I trusting one another or doubting each other's position?"

"Why do you keep asking questions at the end of your statements?"

"Exactly my point! I'm doing it to make sure I'm not missing the answer that God wants me to hear."

"But at some point, you need to have confidence that the question is answered."

"*Trust beyond a doubt?* You're asking me on what is my trust beyond a doubt based?"

"There you go with the questions again, but yeah, that's what I'm asking."

"Easy. I want to trust in God, but I have difficulty seeing and hearing and even identifying what I believe to be the will of God. I keep wanting to define it to my benefit, my way, my rules. So I have to keep studying and praying and listening with one single thing in mind."

"Which is?"

"My faith beyond a doubt in a God who wants me to have a personal one-on-one relationship with Him. If I refuse to doubt His love for me, I'll have difficulty misplacing my faith for Him by misplacing it m…me.

"You see, this is where I have a problem. Okay, there was a god. Okay, he was all-powerful and all…all-every- thing. But I see no proof that he's interacting with you or me or anyone! You're simply asking me to take your word for the fact that the things happening in your life have some kind of correlation to the existence of a supreme being with whom, you claim, you have an inside pass.

"Doubt beyond trust. Now you want me to prove the basis of my belief beyond a doubt?"

"You're making me crazy, but sure, prove your faith to me beyond a doubt."

"I can't, but you can."

"Another riddle, or are you trying to avoid answering?"

"Here's why I can't. Assuming we're both in agreement that there is one God, not multiple gods—"

"Sure. Fine—"

"Does God go to others to ask them to define Him so He can be their God?"

"I know a lot of people who do that."

"Right, but God doesn't. He is who He is. So how can my faith be your faith? It has to be personal— intimate. I can't make your faith for you by proving my faith. You have to encounter God yourself."

"Wait a minute—if that's true, how will I be able to recognize your god?"

"Oh, if you're really seeking Him and find Him, you will definitely know. That's the trick actually. Lots of people get impatient or want the quick route to meeting God—they want to schedule a therapy session, and once they think they've found Him, they want to box God up and take Him with them, like a wallet or a purse they can keep handy, storing Him so when their stuff happens again, they can pull God

out of their pocket and let Him whoop-up on the stuff. They think God will keep their happy lives safe for them while they go about doing the same things they've always done."

"Your god isn't a wallet—got it."

"But other people want God to paint their lives according to what they think it should look like. Some people want freedom, so they define God as unconditionally loving. Some people want power, so they define God as a giver of strength. Some want wealth, some healing, some want to get even or just want a new life without a painful past."

"So people define a god according to their need at the time, and in doing so, they actually set themselves and others up for unbelief or doubt when things don't go their way?"

"He's not waiting for people to tell Him what they want. He's waiting for them to listen for what He wants, and that's what people hate about a relationship with God.

"That this god was bigger and smarter and better than they are and that they have to follow his instructions. Yeah, I see why that's a pain. I already have parents, and they are a big enough pain, I don't need another one."

"Not just that. I want God, my parents, everyone else to want what I want and to give me what I need— without any strings attached. And while I'm at it, I want everyone to believe the same things I believe— act the same way I act and do as I do, without getting in my way."

"I doubt that you're gonna get your way then."

"Thanks for making my point. I don't get my way, nor are you going to get your way, nor is anyone. We all start off thinking and acting the way I just laid out—selfishly, even when we're trying to be

good boy/girl scouts by accomplishing some wonderful deed. We're in it for some personal agenda."

"That's a seriously skeptical attitude for such a good believer."

"If I were good, if any of us were good, without a doubt, we wouldn't be having this conversation."

"To get good, I need to get in good with a god who you can't define for me? How's that work?"

"*Counterdoubt.*"

CHAPTER FIVE

*If it is true that we have a personal relationship with
God, then that's enough for me.*

From a Radix Magazine interview
Faith and Hope and Rock and Roll
T-Bone Burnett
American songwriter and musician 1948-

"Making up words now are we? Counterdoubt? I can do that too...
milkwrap. See?"

"When we first started this, I asked you if belief in God scared you
and you accused me of using fear tactics for pointing out our friend's
situation there in the parking lot. Let's take him out of it for a second
and tell me honestly. Does the idea of coming face to face with an all-
powerful, perfect God at the end of your life scare you?"

"You first."

"Fair enough. I didn't think about it much until I lost a friend, and
then I thought more about what would happen if I didn't come face to
face with God at the end. What would that be like? Nothing? Just an
end? Or worse, something beyond with no God involved?"

"But that's the whole point—you, I, we all have fears, regardless of whether or not we believe in a god. I don't want to live like that. I want my life full of hopes and dreams—happiness!"

"Me too. That got me thinking how different the fears of believers and unbelievers are. People who doubt God's existence fear the uncontrollable and the unpredictable—physical and spiritual elements that they can't see, but that nonetheless affect their lives. People who have faith in God's existence fear... are in awe of...the Creator—God's total power over those same physical and spiritual elements that they believe they can see."

"But what if you're...what if believers in your god are wrong? What if at the end is just nothing?"

"It wouldn't actually make me or us wrong. We just would have risked everything on nothing. I can tell you, though, that in choosing faith over doubt as my main belief, I've discovered I'm not wrong. I know God exists beyond a shadow of a doubt."

"Wait. Before you said you couldn't prove your doubt beyond trust, but now you say you have belief in a god beyond a shadow of a doubt. Isn't that the same thing, and if so, how? I don't get your absolutism about something that's invisible to me!"

"I've found that, if you believe in something significant—a powerful idea, a man or group with a purpose, God—that something strengthens you, not the other way around."

"But I've known lots of people who say they have faith. T^Ahey're typically very loud about it. Then when it really counts, when they need to act on their faith, they usually don't."

"Back to fearing, that what they have faith in, that He or it doesn't exist—doubt?"

"Yeah, fear is weird that way. I've read articles about people who haven't worked through their belief. When their faith is confronted by the unknown and they sense harm to themselves, they'll either completely deny the option of any faith, or they'll try to associate themselves with the faith with which they're most familiar. It might be from a childhood exposure or something they read."

My fear is that this guy is making some sense and I'll have to spend all day arguing my points. I wish this kind of discussion could happen when there was no time limit!

"**Your point being that they have weak faith and, when pressed, they'll abandon the belief out of panic or in search of something else to protect them?**"

"Right. They're completely noncommittal until something bad happens, and then—"

"**They don't know what to believe in. Possibly like Ambulance Guy—sure hope he had it straight beforehand. What about you?**"

"Yeah, I hope he did too."

"**No, I mean, what about you? Do you want to wait till the last minute to deal with your doubt, or do you want to have your faith screwed on tight before the inevitable?**"

"I'm not convinced by what you just explained that having rock-solid faith in a god would make a difference. You still have fear."

"**Yup, but I'm afraid of something completely different than what lies beyond. My fear is that I've not spent the time I should getting to know God, looking for ways to respond to His love each minute I continue to breathe. The odd thing is, the longer I'm doing those things, the less fearful I become and the more protected...loved...I feel.**"

"How do you keep count? How do you know you're doing enough?"

"**I don't keep count—don't need to. My accomplishments are in spite of me, not because of me. It's my focus that counts. If I'm not focused on my faith in God, I'm stressed. He might even remind me from time to time—lots of times—when I forget my focus. If I'm focused on my faith in God, I'm looking in the right direction. I know I can get through anything— do anything—depending on His guidance.**"

"Because your god made you somehow special?"

"**Oh no, that's the other mistake I've made, thinking I'd become important and powerful because of my faith in God. My faith will never make me any more special than I already was before I accepted the reality of God in my life. The only thing that allows for my improvement is God's faith in me.**"

"I get that. Like I was saying about people I saw in church, they seemed to put too much faith in their

faith, believing that their belief in a god caused their god to become more powerful and that—because they believed in him—they could claim anything they did was for him."

"Almost as if their faith had created God and they controlled His will instead of the other way around?"

"And that's why I have so much trouble with anyone who claims they're a strong believer in anything— whether it's a god or a government or… anything. They all believe they're the source of the faith and as its creator, they can define it any way they want!"

"They all believe that way?"

"I guess that is an overstatement on my part. There might be people out there who are sincere in their beliefs, and if their faith is in a god—if they're committed to seeking the truth of that god—they might be Okay. But how do you know when someone is following their god and not using his name to promote their own agenda?"

"I'm not about to claim that I can tag anyone as being sincere or indifferent about their innermost spiritual relationship. Honestly, I have doubts about most people and whether or not they're true *followers* of their professed faiths."

"Well, you've sure heard my side of doubt about you followers, so you won't get any argument from me!"

"For that matter, I know a number of *God deniers* and *God doubters*—serious unbelievers—who still appear to have some unexplained curiosity about the higher spiritual aspects of life."

"Okay, you nailed me there."

"Then who am I to deny you the opportunity to explore further that internal yearning that seems hardwired into you and all humankind? Let me ask you something else. Are you ready to meet God right now?"

"Like an appointment? Does he have a secretary? How's next Tuesday? Wait, you're not going to do the gun routine again and take me to meet your god, are you?"

"Funny. No, no one can take you or force you to meet God, you have to put aside your fears and let Him come to you—on His terms."

"Really—I've never been afraid of meeting anyone—why should I be afraid to meet your god? I guess if someone tried to introduce me to an ax murderer in a dark alley, that would be pretty scary, but God wasn't ever an ax murderer, was he?"

"No. But you just brought up another great point. If you're truly not afraid of encountering God, what else could you possibly be afraid of?"

"I don't know. Maybe the dark when I was a kid. And that ax murderer showing up at my door."

"Things that go bump in the night. Images of pain that no one can protect you from. Images like you probably had when I was reaching for my flashlight."

"You really freaked me out, you know that?"

"Sorry, but here's the point, God knows that because we're trapped in our thinking, having to constantly compare things to figure out if they are good or evil. Not doubting is an impossible task for us on our own. So He gave us a tool, a weapon actually, against the unknown. Counterdoubt—the ability to consider the unseen unapproachable—trusting in spite of the inability to see or approach. Some people call it belief, others call it faith."

"Before this morning, I always thought faith was the opposite of doubt, not something that existed alongside it."

"So did I, but if you think about it, you or I can have very strong faith in something or someone and also possess equally strong doubt of its existence. You proved it with your very convincing arguments about not believing in God when, deep down, you suspect He does exist."

"Ouch. So how do I build c.ounterclou...faith, while having so much doubt getting in the way?"

"You don't. Faith is given to you. It's a gift that you either accept or reject. Then it's simply a question of living it out—applying it to see God in the world around you. If you use it all the time, no matter what's happening or being said around you, God becomes very easy to define and understand and...well, to see."

"You've seen your god?"

"I see Him working."

"How do you know it was your god's work and not just some freak accident of chance or for that matter, some do-gooder who unintentionally gets it right?"

"When you practice cynicism or doubt a lot, you get better and better at spotting suspicious actions, don't you?"

"That's true."

"Same thing with faith—look at our guy out there. The *doubter* in me would be convinced that he hasn't got a prayer—they've been working on him too long. But *faithful me* sees God at work."

"How so, what have you seen your god doing? Because, I'd think your god would have either turned off the switch already or had Ambulance Guy doing cartwheels to help you prove your point."

"I think God is using the situation to give us a focal point. It all adds up."

"Your god using that guy's pain and suffering to help us in a coffee room chat? That is ax murderer stuff!"

"Not exactly. It is, however, one of the really tough lessons I still struggle with as a believer."

"I believe that!"

"I'm learning to look for God's purpose versus my preference in everything I see around me—to recognize where He's working, and love Him. My choice— no matter what."

"That *no matter what* is the sticking point. What if I don't trust that this god of yours has done what's best?"

"Yeah, it sure can look that way to me too. I've put a lot of faith in more of my solutions than those I believe are God's. But when I look back, my solutions always seem to eventually have fallen apart and caused more harm than good."

"Sure, but if you honestly backtrack and ran through what you think your god would have done, would the outcome have been any better?"

"That's the key of faith. Yes, I believe whatever purpose He had, and still has in mind, was and is the best, no matter what."

"Well, that sure provides an excuse if the outcome looks bad. Then you can blame it on your god and not accept any of the responsibility yourself. Isn't that just a way to justify your own actions?"

"Can be, and I've done that—I'm learning not to though. If I have faith in God, then I have to be ready to claim His outcomes as my outcomes and accept the consequences—trusting in His love for the world… and for me. It doesn't mean the world will judge me well, but it does mean that I've not gotten in the way of the one power in the universe that actually can foresee and act out the best solution."

"The problem is that, by that kind of standard, you're talking about some long-term planning, and you may not live long enough to see those results. How will you know your god has done the best things?"

"Again, it's all about putting faith in Him and putting my doubt in all other options, including my own."

"Putting doubt in anything but your god—I hadn't thought of it in those terms."

"God wants us to know who is God and love Him willingly, no matter what."

"Why would I want to love a god who had worked that way? You talk about doubt versus faith—I doubt a god who had acted through pain was a god of love."

"Interesting that you would pose the question that way. I had to ask myself the same question another way, with a condition on the beginning, for it to make sense. If God is the most powerful force in the universe and if He does want a relationship, wouldn't He want the most powerful of relationships—the best of all worlds?"

"So the question is really not why would I want to love a god like that?, but how would an all-powerful god want me to love him?'"

"I know we tried you out in the role of a god. Stepping back into the *big boots* again, can you tell me how, as a god, you would want to be loved?"

"I'd…I wouldn't want to force it, you know…I'd want to be loved for who I am."

"Faithfully?"

"Faithfully is good."

"Don't you think God-who-is-not-you might want the same thing?"

"Then why do I hear about churches and mosques and groups promoting a forced choice belief in their god, insisting that I believe in their god, some religions even selling the idea that they are their god's personal instrument to punish, or kill those who don't believe as that group does?"

"Yeah, some think that people must believe in God or suffer an immediate punishment, but those groups have missed out on faith beyond fear—fear is only a reaction to the unknown. When somebody truly gets to know God intimately...deeply, then suddenly, fear turns to respectful awe. That's the beginning of the real relationship, and no one can force that kind of love to happen, it has to be desired."

"That's why I've fought with belief in a god. Because everyone else expects me to believe, and if I don't, they stick their nose up at me, or they threaten that their god will fry me. They make faith a requirement of everyone, believer and unbeliever, and the irony is, they don't even have enough faith in their faith to allow others to live with their own choices, good or bad."

"You base your choice to have a relationship with God on other people's faults? How odd, I thought that faith was a personal choice, not based on others' beliefs or actions."

"Touche."

"I do agree with one thing others claim. Since faith is a gift from God, you can't believe in God without faith."

"But that doesn't mean I can't have faith in something besides a god. I have faith in gravity for instance. I can't see it, but I don't go around grabbing hold of things because I think suddenly I'm going to float away."

"Right, and you don't go around questioning whether or not gravity exists. You don't attack the very thing that keeps you grounded. Those who discover that God does exist discover new spiritual realities much like the physical realities that we shape our lives around."

"You're driving at something."

"Before I understood gravity, I asked, why do I not float away? Now that I recognize gravity, I ask, what does gravity allow me to do?"

"Unless you're a kid who wants to explore—you know, climb trees— then you find out that gravity is no good. It hurts when you fall. So you become afraid of it."

"Or *very* respectful of it. Gravity shouldn't stop you from climbing trees—it's there to help keep you in the tree."

"So?"

"So as I break through the barrier of my personal doubt that leads to my spiritual faith, the foundation of my questions change from what if God doesn't exist? to what if God does exist?"

"But that suggests, for me to have spiritual faith, there would have been a god who created spiritual faith in the first place, like gravity has existed, even though I didn't know what it was or how it worked."

"You're catching on, but there is one big difference between gravity and faith I've failed to mention."

"I'm waiting—"

"Gravity is a law without choice. Faith is a gift to be accepted or rejected."

"That's heavy."

"And speaking of feeling weighted down, this tired old body of mine is telling me I've got to stand up and stretch for a minute."

"Speaking of bodies, I wonder if they're making progress in the ambulance?"

"Hard to tell. I'd go out there and see if I could offer some comfort to our guy, but they've already turned several people away. I think they want some space. You know what? That brings up a very good point."

"What's that?"

"I don't know if those paramedics out there are well trained. I've never seen their credentials, and from in here, I can't see them working on our guy in the ambulance."

"Go on."

"I have no idea if they can help or not. I just have to trust based on my previous observations of medical personnel. I have to believe in them even if I don't completely comprehend their abilities."

"Quaint. You're drawing an analogy to how you have to trust in your god even if you can't see him at work."

"No, not at all. I'm suggesting that God is God, whether I believe He exists or not, and God will do what God will do, not based on my perceptions of His skill of being God."

"Gee, you're lucky your god lets you hang around to watch. He could snuff you out along with Ambulance Guy."

"You can be sarcastic, but the truth is, I do believe He could easily do just that. The fact that He doesn't—that He still wants to have a relationship with someone like me, who has doubted His existence so strongly—proves His incredible patience and love for me...for us."

"All I know is that my legs are starting to cramp up from sitting so much. How'bout I stretch with you and walk to the counter. This time, I'll buy, but don't go pulling out any inappropriate weapons, even flashlights. Okay?"

"I won't turn that offer down. On the way, tell me...have you ever fallen in love?"

CHAPTER SIX

I self destruct every relationship so that i don't get hurt…
but in truth i just hurt myself worse in the long run.

Anonymous

"So you love someone, not an immediate family member, but you know, someone special?"

"Yeah."

"Describe them to me."

"You mean physically?"

"I mean how you see them. If that makes you uncomfortable, you don't have to, I'll understand."

"No, that's fine, I don't mind at all. She's, well, beautiful, in lots of ways. She's got auburn hair. It goes down to the middle of her back, but she usually has it, uh, pinned somehow—in kind of a loose knot. I don't know how she does it."

"Go on. Is she smart?"

"Rocket science smart? No way! But smart in a…a watchful sort of way. She can peg people. You know what I mean? She can tell you what you're thinking, what you're gonna do before you even know."

"That might be a little unnerving."

"Yeah, but in a cool kind of way. It's nice knowing someone is that interested in you…in me—wants to know me that well."

"What does she like to do?"

"She's a reader, reads everything. And she likes to walk. At least she says she likes to, says that helps her keep in shape, but I think she really likes to listen and talk. Walking is just a way to not be distracted and to be alone."

"With you?"

"Yeah, alone with me—she likes that. I like that."

"You sound very happy describing her."

"I do? I.I am! I love her. A lot! I enjoy talking about her. It makes me feel close to her right now."

"I totally understand that feeling. I feel the same about my wife, even after a large number of years together. Love really focuses you on another person."

"That's a good way to describe it. I can tell you as much or more about her than I can about any other person I know."

"Not just about her physical appearance, but about her character and spirit."

"Yeah, right, those too. She's my *center*!"

"As in *center of your universe*?"

"Yeah, that's it. Center of my universe."

"She sounds very special, you're very blessed."

"Yeah. Thanks."

"Before you met her, did you have an idea in your mind that someone like her was out there? Did you start searching for her?"

"Where are you going with this? Do you want me to start dating your god?"

"Only if you know a really nice place to take Him…kidding. Back to your *special someone*, *how* did you know your someone was *the one*?"

"The what? Oh, I liked what I saw, I guess."

"And you knew what you wanted and what you wanted them to be, right?"

"OK?"

"**When you met your someone, you compared what you wanted them to be, to what they are, and suddenly you were in love?**"

"Kind of."

"**But how did you know what love was? How did you even know you wanted to be in love?**"

"I guess I saw other people in love and thought I want that too."

"**How did you know they were really in love?**"

"Oh, come on, you've seen people in love, they do really strange things!"

"**Like?**"

"Like hanging around the person all the time and doing whatever they think the other person wants and listening to the person and buying them flowers, that stuff, but what has this got to do with your god?"

"**Sounds like a lot of work. Again as you said, high maintenance.**"

"Both for the one who wants to love and for the one who wants to be loved, but does the one who wants to be loved really have to make it more work than necessary?"

"**Stupid, isn't it? Why make something harder than it has to be?**"

"You're trying to use my words against your god against me? That doesn't fly. Human relationships are totally different."

"**Oh? How so?**"

"I can touch my someone—flesh and blood—duh! I'm sorry, I think I get the *faith angle*, but even if I did start seeing an active god having been at work out there, I still don't buy into the touchy feely *god-inside- me* thing that you Christians and some other religions seem so convinced of."

"**Seems to me if bacteria and viruses and other living things can inhabit me physically, why can't I cohabitate with spiritual beings as well?**"

"I don't think there's anything but *me* in me. I am who I am. Your god is maybe on the same bus, but two separate seats, fine, and maybe your god's the driver."

"**Doesn't sound very intimate—you and God— you get off at your stop and He just keeps moving on.**"

"Yeah well, think positive, at least you got me to admit I'm taking the bus. Like you said, lots of people don't even bother with the ride."

"Ever think of following Him home to see what He does in His free time?"

"Come on man, I don't have time for…"

"Okay, Okay, listen, I know we've been all into our guy on the gurney out there, but look in here. See that woman over there pouring through the fiction section? What about Emo-boy with all the tattoos digging pennies out of his pocket for some juice? And then there's the two weird ones sitting at the table cradling their coffees and peering casually at a possible passing of life right outside the window at which they sit."

"Now you're getting personal."

"It has always been personal. That's the thing God wants most."

"If that's so, if this god was that hot of a commodity and so great, why aren't you, why isn't everyone, lining up to be his best buddy?"

"Who says most aren't? Again with the backwards thinking— mine, yours, most people's problem is that we start with 'God, be my buddy, hang with me—let me show you a good time…I'll even buy.' If I don't like the way things are going, I can move on to another better-looking or more compatible date."

"But why would a god want to…date you or me in the first place?"

"Can an all-powerful being do an all-powerful thing, focusing on it as something worth loving, making it the center of His universe?

"But I don't get the point of—"

"And if the Creator of the universe would want this thing, could He foresee all the obstacles, contingencies, consequences, and the final outcome of such a relationship? Oh, by the way, are you happy with your someone?"

"What? Yeah."

"Is she perfect?"

"Yeah, well, no…for me she is. Sure we have our moments, when we don't see eye-to-eye, but we work it out"

"Wouldn't it be great if God loved you the way you love her?"

"Yeah, but love is an emotion. I don't think your god had emotions."

"Oh, God doesn't have feelings?"

"That's it. Why should he? He was a god. He could do anything he wanted."

"**Wait, anything He wants? He can desire?**"

"Fine, he had that emotion."

"**If He can have one, why not others. How do you know He doesn't have other emotions?**

"I just see what I see. If there was a god that cared, he'd really have cared."

"**Oh, like you mean.care for you? You want God to demonstrate another emotion, care.**"

"Yeah, for starving people and people who were hurting and—"

"**And the world, like for Ambulance Guy? Speaking of—I wonder who else Ambulance Guy is thinking about out there?**"

"Are you joking? His family, friends, whoever!"

"**Can he depend on them?**"

"I don't know—why not?"

"**Divorce, breakups, arguments, carelessness—**"

"We all have that in our lives, if we can't depend on those people, I'm sorry—you can't keep me from believing in my family. They're the only ones I have."

"**Or don't have. You're right. Everyone hopes they can lean on those closest to them in a crisis, but what if they let us down, or what if we've chased them away?**"

"Really—has that happened to you? Didn't you say something like your god throws you people to hang on to, like a rope to help pull you up when you're in the pit?"

"**God does that, yes.**"

And continues to do it for me. Why can't I get him to see how actively involved You are, even in this conversation?

"You know, God can let you down too."

"**Really—has that happened to you?**"

"*Not visible* equals *not helping*. That's how I see it."

"**Strange choice of words, but shine a light on the idea—is God letting down Ambulance Guy out there? Does God abandon us, or is it the other way around?**"

"Well, from what I see out that window, your god looks guilty as charged. If Ambulance Guy is looking for help, why isn't *Supreme Guy* helping him?"

"How do you know He isn't?"

"Still in ambulance, still not moving. Duh again!"

"I get it, you want to see God in action, an immediate fix, a…a miracle!"

"Sure. Why not a miracle? If your god is so great and if he's so into relationships, why doesn't he just fix that guy right now?"

"Maybe miracles aren't intended for people without faith. Maybe they're meant as a gift to those who have faith, part of an intimate dance of spiritual love. To dance the dance, you have to hear the music. The more you practice the dance together, the more beautiful the result."

"Oh, you're laying it on me—if that guy is going to recover, I have to believe in your god enough, and if I don't believe enough, the guy is history?"

"That sounds like the makings of a great guilt trip to me. I sure wouldn't want that dumped on me!"

"Me either, so back off."

"Wow! Sounds like someone in your history tried that already—that was a pretty angry response. Besides, that's not what I'm suggesting at all."

"So you've loved your god that way—danced with him, what—your whole life?"

"No, in my universe, I failed at loving God."

"You've lost me again."

"I blew it. I had once thought as you do now, that God was some distant thing, not interested in me. So I stopped being interested in Him. Instead, I chose to be judge and jury of my world. I was all too happy to point out how sucky the world was, and I could tell you exactly which miserable people had made it that way."

"If the world is such a sucky place, and I've done my own share of criticizing, I still don't get what that has to do with loving a god."

"To love God, I first had to love what God created. I didn't know love's origin, so I couldn't understand love's purpose."

"That's haiku BS."

"Dommo arigato."

"Love alone should be purpose enough."

"Why not, let's go with *love alone*. You want a relationship, you know who you want it with, you jump in with both feet. Then suddenly, the someone you love says, 'I want to be the main one in your life. I want the best of what you are, and I'll share with you the best of what I am.'"

"I totally get that. If I'm not willing to share the best and worst of what I am with the one I really want to love, and if I'm not willing to do some compromising—"

"Sacrificing?"

"Sure, sacrificing, then I'm not really committed to making that relationship work."

"Sounds like you've had some experience at this. So what if you started having actual conversations with this God you've just decided exists, and what if He asked that of you, could you give it to Him?"

"Sorry again, I don't see anyone doing that, not even your god."

"Not at all?"

"Well, not much. I see you waving your hands, but that doesn't prove anything."

"Why not?"

"Because I don't think there's much evidence that this god of yours talks to people, unless you include legends and stories 'ancl...cr'azy people."

"And people who wave their hands around in bookstores."

"That's you talking to your god, not your god talking to you.

"Oh? What makes you so sure of that?"

"We're back to that? There's a secret radio transmitter in your head and you're hearing voices? That falls into the *crazy people* category."

"Is the box you keep God in that small? What if God didn't just use voices in the head, or not just lightning on smoking mountaintops? Do you think that's the only way He's capable of getting people's attention or even communicating?"

"Maybe I've just been watching too many movies, but those seem to be the standard *MO* that people recite when they've heard from the *Big Guy*."

"Probably because you've heard that coming from people who want other people to be impressed. What would be more earth shattering to you, a thunderclap from heaven or a small, still voice in your head that

whispers your name? What if God spoke to each person in different ways? How do you figure out if God does or doesn't talk to people?"

"Well, that's the trick, isn't it? If you don't want to believe in a god, you won't hear a god. If you do want to believe in a god, you're going to want to hear that god. And if you don't hear your god, you'll want to so badly that you'll actually believe that you do hear. Like Almost Dead Guy out there—he needs a miracle bigtime, so I bet he's suddenly hearing all kinds of strange stuff in his head. If your god loves him, let your god prove it. You know, *walk the walk.*"

"Not just *talk the talk*. Well, there's got to be a way to test your theory out, to make sure whoever really is hearing does something about it. I know I'd want that kind of validation if people were saying they were hearing from God. Wouldn't you?"

"Sure, but how?"

"Hey, I've got an idea. Let's pray together, right now for a miracle for Ambulance Guy. Come on, you start, and I'll help out."

"Hold it. I'm not into that *out loud prayer* thing."

"Are you into the *to yourself prayer* thing?"

"Look, I'm only now coming to terms with the possibility of a god being out there, and besides, why do we have to ask him for a miracle, why doesn't he just do it?"

"You said you wanted proof."

"I did?"

"Yeah, you said you wanted to see God in action. You said 'why not a miracle—*walk the walk*?' That's asking for proof. If you want proof, you've got to go looking for it. If you're looking for it, you go to the source of it. If you're going to the source, that would be God because you're asking Him to prove Himself, right?"

"Okay."

"And if you're asking Him, that's communication. That would mean you have to, oh, I don't know...talk with Him? I think they call that prayer."

"But that guy out there is the one who should be asking for proof, not me."

"Oh, each according to their need, right? Well, maybe he is praying. Maybe he's real weak and hurt, maybe he needs our help because he

hasn't ever done this before and doesn't know how to pray. Maybe he's just scared or too proud to ask for help. Maybe he's only now coming to terms with the possibility of God being out there, and besides, why should he have to ask for a miracle, why doesn't God just do it?"

"I was just about to say that's his and his god's problem, but you're telling me it's my problem?"

"I thought you said you wanted to make a difference, do something good?"

"I did, but praying seems so useless!"

"Useless? Really, how much practice have you had at it?"

"I hate you more."

"No doubt. Come on, what's the harm? Ready to talk to Him?"

"No."

"Why not? You said you wanted God to care, but you don't care?"

"Look, you're the one convinced that it will help.

You do it." "I am. That's the waving hands, talking to someone who isn't here thing you think is so weird."

"Not helping, is it?"

"You were the one wanting to pray for a miracle of instant healing. You don't know what I'm praying for."

"Well? What are you praying for?"

"I'll tell you a little later. Do you still want your prayer answered?"

"I'll tell you a little later."

"You've said there could be a God. Maybe, just maybe, He does exist, and He might be the one with expectations, not me."

"You actually think that if I prayed for Ambulance Guy to get well immediately that it would happen?"

"I don't know. I do know that two things would have to happen before that."

"What two things?"

"One, you would have to absolutely believe that the God you were praying to has the ability to do what you're asking. And two, you'd have to put God's wants before your wants."

"Listen, I think your god has done whatever your god wanted to do with or without my input, so talking to him really doesn't excite me. Just sounds like another thing for us to have to agree to disagree on."

"Cop-out!"

"Excuse me?"

"You heard me. We all do that when we don't want to confront or commit. We say 'Let's just all get along with our different ideas' to evade making each other uncomfortable. And the choice is then made for us. We have no real relationship at all. We exist together in a world of...nothing. Then I make a decision that may affect you negatively, maybe even ending your physical life before you're ready to go. If I don't permanently off you, maybe you resent my decision. I anger or offend you. You choose altercation or retaliation or escalation or whatever you want to call it, and suddenly we're at war—all because we agree to disagree. It's a cop-out, and I'm tired of not agreeing."

"Get over it."

"I am getting over it. Right now, right here. I'm sharing my deepest thoughts and fears and hopes, my soul and my spirit, with another human being. It's not to change you, it changes me, it causes me to look deeper into God's purpose for me."

"Lovely. Are you changed now? Can I go?"

"I'm not the one who makes that choice. Let me ask you just one more question though, how does a deep intimacy really begin?"

"Uh, there has to be some form of connection. Maybe at first unspoken, but then a communication that can survive even the breaking of the initial bond, even if a significant argument comes up or other competing relationships try to interfere."

"Could that communication be nonverbal, possibly symbolic or written?"

"What? Like a love letter, gifts, a candy gram from You-Know-Who?"

"Ways of letting the loved one know they're loved. It would have to be easy and deep, but interesting, even fun, and sometimes, very serious. There would have to be romance too—can't have love without romance. Those are the things that become the best memories and help me...love back."

"Hmmm, almost sounds like the premise for some epic tome."

"I wonder if it would sell?"

"You're getting in over your head. You're obviously talking about a relationship of biblical proportions. Your question to me simply suggested how a deep humanistic relationship begins."

"Was it? I don't recall making that distinction, and what if there isn't a difference? Could you imagine

how incredibly strong and beautiful our human relationships would be were we to treat them as sacred, sacrificing voluntarily and holding on to that love, no matter what happens?"

"Point taken. The problem I see is that most relationships don't hold up over time. We get bored, or I don't know, we want stuff the other person just can't give."

"Like?"

"It's different in each relationship. We just aren't ever satisfied."

"Maybe because we're still comparing and not trusting?"

"Back to the choice issue?"

"Intimacy starts that way—choosing to have belief in the other, or choosing to have faith only in yourself. You can't really see inside the other person's thoughts. You have to trust that they have your best interest at heart. If you don't offer that trust, the only things left are anticipation or suspicion."

"Are they with me or against me?"

"If you get in the habit of thinking like that, you're forced to choose each day—whether or not to agree or disagree with the arrangement. Since it's an everyday resolution, there's no long-term commitment, only a temporary contract."

"But if I don't compare the relationships I start, how will I know the ones worth pursuing?"

"Comparisons—*good* versus *bad*—equal disagreement. Because, there is no resolution, leading to no commitment, resulting in no true...permanent relationship—no commitment."

"Comparisons, relationships, wait! I just put it together—you're suggesting that the meaning of the two is almost identical. If I don't compare, there is no relationship, so how would two people come together?"

"They would agree. They would seek...unity. They would be totally and inseparably intimate."

"But you'd have to know ahead of time that the *whoever* was the one whoever that you wanted to love. How would you know that?"

"This is where the trail splits in how God and human relationships go. God knows and wants me to know Him. Unfortunately, since I want to measure and compare things, I have to measure and compare my relationship to God with other relationships instead of simply trusting in Him."

"But how can I—?"

"You can't! That's what I'm trying to get through to you. God wants it, so He creates it, not you. If you believe He created everything else, then you have to believe that He's created the way for you to love Him."

"And I just have to *choose* to love? That's it? There's got to be more to it than that. I need to think about it before I can seriously agree to that choice."

"Fair enough. Choice is still what this is all about. But while you're trying to wrap your head around that, stop searching for more relationships, start getting intimate with your *first love.*"

"Don't worry, I'm so confused now I don't want to muddy the waters. I'm going to make sure I have everything worked out with her before—"

"Her? Hold on, have you been having some kind of out-of-body experience during this conversation? Did you think by first love I meant your someone?"

"Well…yeah!"

"I meant get intimate with God. He was the *Someone-before-your-someone* and loves you passionately. Get your passion for Him straight before you explore passion with anyone else."

"Passion? How can anyone get passionate with a Creator of the known universe? That's far-fetched at best!"

"I confess, it's the strangest paradigm out there, God being more eager than I am to share private time with me. What would you say to God if He were sitting in the chair across from you?"

"Oh, oh, now you're the god?"

"I wanted the position, but I wasn't and never will be in any way up to the job. No, I'm not God, and there are really two reasons to get your relationship down with Him before anything else."

"Because?"

"Because, if you get that relationship right, you get the rest of them right."

"I know lot's of people who call themselves *believers* who've failed at other relationships."

"I didn't say discovering the disease cures the illness. Getting it right with God takes a lifetime. I have a lifetime to work on it. The question is, how long is that lifetime?"

"Which I suspect leads to your other reason? Go ahead, explain it to me, I need to get my relationship right with a god because?"

"Because we're all Ambulance Guy just waiting to happen. At some moment in time, you, me, everyone in this store, and everyone out there beyond the parking lot will crash. The question is, how ready am I for that moment?"

"Back to the *Am I ready to date your god* question?"

"More like moving on to the *Is God ready to date you* question. What would you talk about?"

"Are you kidding? First, I'd ask why he bothered to set up this crazy scheme. Then I'd ask about why I can't understand math while my sister is a calculus wiz. Then, well, there'd be a bunch of stuff. I'd want to know how to end war, and hunger, and—"

"But what would He want to talk about?"

"What?"

"You seem to think you'd have a lot of important things to chat about. Don't you think the Creator of the known universe might want to share a few tidbits too?"

"Of course your god would have something to say. That's why churches and religious groups are supposed to be out there, to hear the *Word* and turn it into something that helps out. The problem I see is in those groups claiming ownership, control, over what their god has to say."

"You have that correct. The Word isn't supposed to validate a group's purpose, it's there to invite the group to join a higher purpose."

"So what group has it right? Who are the *best* believers?"

"I could tell you the obvious about my belief, and I could start telling you about why I believe the way I do, but that would be my *why*, me sharing my faith and trying to make it yours. Wouldn't it be

better if you started to intimately and passionately start talking to God—better yet, listening for however He might be talking to you? Wouldn't that be God's existence intimately proving itself to you?"

"But how can you test what's right? If you don't first see it working somewhere else, how do you know what your god is doing and who else he's doing it with?"

"Before I can share faith, I have to have faith. Belief isn't a consensus, it begins and ends individually—intimately."

"But if belief ends just as it begins—so intimately— why share faith with anyone else in the world?"

CHAPTER SEVEN

So I wanted to sing inspirational music, and that's exactly how I approached it—

only the words have been changed to declare my relationship with God.

From the 2004 interview *Miracle Man—*
|Smokey Robinson
American songwriter and musician 1940-

"How's our boy out there? And speaking of someone in real need, here's a question. If you had, or knew, something that would help him, would you?"

"Give me a *for-instance.*"

"Say they were stepping on his oxygen hose and you saw it, but they didn't, would you intervene?"

"Yeah, of course."

"Even though you're not a health professional? What if they didn't see the error and didn't believe you? What if they were really busy working on him and didn't want to mess with you. What if they told you to bug off?"

"I'd show them anyway."

"And not agree to disagree?"

"Different. That's *life-or-death* stuff out there."

"What if this stuff in here is life-or-death stuff?"

"It's not. Look, your precious Bible even contradicts itself in the first couple of chapters. It says something about your god telling Adam and Eve that if they bite the apple or whatever it is, that they'll die, and look, they didn't!"

"Wait a minute—you buy into the Bible version of creation?"

"Of course not, but I figure it's a good example about how the book doesn't work, and if the book doesn't work from the very beginning, why trust the rest of it?"

"Can I ask you a dangerously sensitive question?"

"I've got thick skin, go for it."

"If that were your someone out there on the gurney, would you be praying to a god, other than yourself?"

"You're right, it is a dangerous question. Let me get back to you on that."

"What if you were Ambulance Guy out there? You've already said that, if you were him, you'd believe in God because you'd want to cover your bases."

"No harm in that. If something happened, I could always cover that base then."

"Oh? What if you're wrong, what if you or I decide to put off making a belief commitment? What if— at the moment you or I, or Ambulance Guy need to make that decision—we can't make that decision?"

"Come on, the fear thing again? What happens if a meteor falls out of the sky and pops me on the head? I'll take my chances, my choice. Besides, you've already said that nothing happens, life goes on."

"Physical life as we know it goes on until it doesn't. Then what? Define death for me?"

"Uh, no breathing, cold slab, I'm history, the world goes on.

"Back to the same question. What if you're wrong? What if death isn't just a physical thing? What if there's another kind of death that happens, where we die when there's an absence of a convicted...a sincere belief in God. What if Adam and Eve died in a.dif- ferent way?"

"I'm not alive because I don't shout 'I believe in God' to everyone who walks by?"

"I don't care if you're shouting or dancing on the table. As a matter of fact, it shouldn't matter to you how strong my belief in God is either. The only one who really needs to know if you and I are sincere in our belief is God."

"Great. For a minute there I was feeling like a character out of that zombie movie. What was it, *Night of the Living Dead?*"

"That's actually closer to the truth than you realize. I used to tell myself everything would magically work itself out in the end without my having to do anything differently. I found out that, if I'm not committed, actually live out what's really true, then I am a walking dead guy."

"*Really true*? I'll bite. What's really true?"

"Even though I've done some good things in my life, none of it counts without God's love in my life. I can't have God's love in my life unless I ask God to forgive me for the crappy things I've done. Once I sincerely admit that to myself and God, then He can start working on the next step."

"Next step? What is this, some kind of twelve-step thing? Sorry, I know there are things I've got to change in my life, but I'm doing pretty well with that. Are you suggesting my efforts aren't good enough?"

"Honestly, I haven't seen one person—including myself, or a government, or a world order—that can effect real change without first wantonly or forcibly being changed by the Changer."

"The Changer—that would be...?"

"That would be the Changer this conversation has been about all along. Look, I don't have to like the fact that I'm not a capable changer of my circumstances, or embrace the idea that I need changing. It's simply...true. And that points me toward an uncomfortable line of difficult self-questioning. If there is a Higher Power inviting me to change, it suggests that I'm in need of the change. I'm.flawed. I've proven it over and over again. You've even pointed out what a mess humanity is.

"Busted again."

"Begging the next question, Am I willing to admit that I'm flawed?, which leads to the ultimate question, Am I willing to recognize and be changed by a power so great that it rids me of every flaw?"

"So I admit I'm a bad boy and that I need help, then what, your god sends me to the corner for *time-out*, then suddenly I'm a good boy?"

"I'm not here to convince or change you. I'm simply here to tell you that I've been changed. The change I speak of isn't something I care to debate, just like my need to be changed. It simply *is*. It's such a great change that I can't help but share my experience And that I've just done."

"Thanks for the bonding moment. What's step 2?"

"For starters, climb the first step—it's the big one. And it doesn't sound like you're interested, so step 2 won't make any sense at all."

"Excuse my sarcasm. It's just that you keep saying 'it's simply this' and 'it's simply that.' Nothing is that simple, and I'm not about to commit any steps to something that isn't clearly the best path. I simply don't have the time."

"Which is why most people, even those who say they believe in God, don't make it past that point in their belief."

"What—there are believers who don't believe enough?"

"Popular thinking suggests that only those who haven't yet *jumped the fence* fall into the category of *skeptic*. But I think there are a lot of followers of God, even *naturalists*, or *science advocates* and *humanists*— calling themselves *dedicated converts*—who claim they're committed with words, yet don't prove out their commitment by their lifestyle."

"So saying 'I believe' isn't enough. Is there a membership fee—a secret handshake? What do I have to do?"

"It's not what I have to do. It's how I live because of what's been done for me, God actually taking away my faults. My belief, combined with a commitment to actually be a legitimate example of that belief, is what God is looking for."

"Your... *believement*."

"My be-what-ment?"

"*Believement*—that's what you just defined. A way of living that proves out your belief. If you just believe something, but don't act it out, you don't really believe it."

"Look at that. Just when I thought I was teaching you something, you teach me."

He's getting it! Now what do I do, how do I break down the barrier to help him over the line?

"I guess I just haven't bought into the commitment thing yet—found a belief to base my believement on. I'm stuck on the point that there seem to be a lot of good ideas out there, and I don't believe any one group has a patent on the best ones. I'm going to have to seek out my own truth."

"Whatever you do, when you start, don't ever stop seeking truth. It's there to find. The sad thing is someone discovering a part of the truth then becoming complacent and stopping their quest for the complete truth. They base all they see on a small corner of a huge universe that God is ready to share with them, personally and intimately, if they'd only dedicate the time and spirit."

"Speaking of sharing, I've just realized, you've been talking all over the map about your god's greatness, but you really haven't told me anything really *intimate* about your relationship with the *Big Power*."

"I didn't always believe the way I do now, not even close. I have difficulty understanding and describing what switch *switched* in me.

"Come on, try—this is the interesting part."

"As a kid, my family didn't go to church. My dad traveled—good hardworking man, very proud—saw himself as a self-made man. Mom was very bright, but she felt trapped in the house, a homemaker who secretly wanted to be a working professional. She found narcotics and prescription medication as a remedy for her frustration and marital loneliness."

"Yeah, I guess we all have some dysfunction hidden in the closet, huh?"

"There was a lot of tension and denial in the house. We kids were encouraged to explore life for our own answers because, other than being hard and dedicated workers, my parents didn't appear to have deep spiritual convictions to lead them. We were encouraged to read

and study, question and learn all we could with no base of comparison other than our parents' struggle."

"You're saying people have to have deep spiritual convictions to be *normal?*"

"No, not to be normal. I suspect lots of people don't possess that depth. But to be healthy—not just physically, I'm talking about completely healthy and fulfilled in life—yeah, you have to dive into the spiritual pool."

"I'm not even sure my pool has enough water in it for a dive."

"That was our problem as a family too. We appeared successful on the outside—just like all the other middle class folk around us. But inside, we were just cynics, wondering at the true purpose of life. I started off with that cynicism as my base. Not just questioning but trying to tear down anything that smacked of authority or established order. I was a rebel for the sake of rebellion only."

"So what changed you?"

"It didn't really seem like a change until it happened. I was invited to come to play guitar in a band. They practiced at a church, and when I heard some of the things they were saying and singing, inwardly I laughed at them. Being who I was, I set out to prove them and their God wrong. I wanted to expose them to be as faulty as I was. The more I looked into their lives and beliefs though, the more I saw...truth. I found, when I was totally honest about it, I couldn't argue away God. He started making sense."

"You drank the lemonade."

"Maybe, but that's when I realized it wasn't their efforts really making the difference. Actually, a lot of those people back then weren't the greatest role models for Christian life either."

"Just like I pointed out before."

"Right. And as I said, it wasn't them doing the changing. They were just examples of what could be done with questionable material. What I discovered was that God was active and at work—changing them, changing me. I suddenly...this is where it gets weird— "

"Let me guess. You *felt* your god's presence."

"More than that. I recognized He had been there all along, not just suddenly appearing, but I could see His spiritual fingerprints all

over my past. He had been preparing for me to come up to the altar of acceptance, and I knew I had to make a choice."

"To believe in your god?"

"Actually I had to decide to believe completely in God, or completely not believe. That's the reality of the barrier. You can't straddle between the two, right or wrong, make the choice.

"And because you made that choice, now you believe…in a different way?"

"Now there is a drive in me to chase God. Before I'd throw out arguments, pointed out other people's philosophies and beliefs that were against God, but sounded noble, just leaving the discussion open-ended. It was safe. Now my life has become strangely dangerous."

"What? Dangerous? How so?"

"Now I know, beyond any doubt, that God exists. I can't not-believe it anymore. There's no recrossing the barrier. It means I've got to live with the understanding that He's involved in my life 24/7. I'm never alone, and anything I say and do affects our relationship."

"Then I'm surprised your God didn't vaporize you when you pulled that gun stunt!"

"Yup, dangerous times we live in. God's grace is the only thing that I know keeps Him and I together."

"So now you're telling me to make that same choice?"

"I'm not telling you to do anything. The question is, what do you hear, not with your ears, but inside you? What or whose voice do you hear when the world is deathly still?"

"I don't know if I've ever really heard that voice."

"I didn't know either. First, I had to stop and listen. Really listen, not just pretend and then come up with my own theories. It was—is still—difficult. I had to begin to…to *chase* it. And one day, I realized that the chase had become a desirable lifestyle. Taking time, practicing, living it and breathing it, acting it out and not just carrying it in a book or throwing it out for casual conversation."

"*Believement.*"

"My *believement.*"

"Well, there you go then, you did just explain it to me. What was so hard about that?"

"**Do you believe as I believe?**"

"No…maybe…I don't know."

"**Do you want to seek God as your first purpose in life? Do you wake up wanting to know more about Him? Do you ask what He would have you do, how He would look at your actions in any given situation? Do you go to bed at night wanting to be more like He wants you to be the next day?**"

"You really do that?"

"**Not enough, but I want to. Each day it's my driving force, my *inside voice*. So each day, I start there, and each day I end there— chasing, running toward, instead of away from God.**"

"And that's it. That's your mountaintop advice. *Run toward your god?* Again, that sounds too simple. And stepping back out of the metaphorical world, into the real one, what does chasing after a god look like anyway?"

"**I'll help you find out. Are you willing to try it?**"

"I'll think it over and get back to you."

"**In other words, it's harder than you think because first, you have to recognize God not just as an entity, or even as a companion, but as a real *lover*.**"

"I'll admit I'm not even sure he's powerful enough— competent to run a small planet, much less the universe."

"**Much less your magnificent existence?**"

"Earlier you asked me about how I'd react if my someone was near death or really hurt. She's my soul mate, and I'd do anything to help her that I could. I think she'd do the same for me, but there's only so much anyone can do. I don't think a god I haven't seen, even if he did exist, would take that much interest in me."

"**If He did, would you start taking a real interest in Him?**"

"I still don't know."

"**Because you can't see?**"

"Right, that's it. Show me your god."

"**Physically you mean? Show you a tangible, touchable version of God?**"

"Yeah, show me that!"

"**Actually I can't, but God can, and did. I believe He actually loved me and you, and everyone so much that He presented Himself** in human form, to be seen and heard and held. He wanted to touch us as much as He hoped we would want to touch Him."

"Oh no, not the *Jesus thing* now—just when I was starting to enjoy this! I'm sorry, but your god having a baby through an *earth mom* and then the baby growing up to be killed and somehow magically brought back to life and sent back to heaven? No way. You're asking too much."

"Jesus Christ is my Savior and Lord, but like I said, I'm not asking you to believe anything. I just told you what I believe. I had big problems with it too then realized there was no other way for God to fix my flaws so that we could have the relationship we do. I don't expect you to understand. Like I said, ***the great and powerful message is really—"***

"Yeah, yeah, I got it, *is really a small and very personal message,* and you're not the one to best explain it. But you still haven't answered my question. Who can explain it?"

"That's the simplest part of all. You can. It's literally between you and God. Believement kept God and me apart, and believement brought us together."

"More haiku. The *barrier* is a bridge?"

"I don't know what language or imagery works for you. I know for me that, once I committed to believing in God, really believing, dedicating my focus and life to Him, things changed. When I became willing to recognize His characteristics, including His willingness to love me enough to sacrifice Himself so that we can have a perfect relationship, I became a totally different person. I wanted different things than I did before—the more I prayed and read and heard about what God desires, the more I was and am

attracted to the lifestyle those desires implied. Now my believement has become the only way I know how to live. It saved—He saved—me from a life of empty, noncommitted rhetoric."

"Look, that works for you, but I have to work through it a little more, you know? The spiritual part and the *saving-me-from-myself* part of this conversation are both just a little too spooky and existential."

"I totally understand. It's sad though."

"What's sad?"

"Listening to you being caught in the middle. I see you actually leaning toward belief in God, but your language suggests that you're more convinced He doesn't exist—every time you've referenced God, it's been in the past tense, never present, with no future hope. You can't seem to make up your mind one way or the other, and so you commit to no belief at all."

"Fine, I'll commit. I don't believe in your god. There, does that help? All you seem to want from me is to for me to get down on my knees and confess my *badness* and then give my life to Jesus. Good grief, all I wanted was a cup of coffee!"

"Do you really believe that?"

"What, that I want coffee?"

"No, that there is no God?"

"Here we go again. Yes! That's what I believe! No… maybe not… damn, will you please just stop that?"

"Stop?"

"Stop testing my convictions. I just don't know, and I'm perfectly satisfied not knowing! Maybe someday that will change, but like your god, I am what I am right now. I guess I just want to be more of that inactive kind of that *inactive* kind of believer you described for the time being."

"Sounds like the conversation's over. I need to be going anyway. Good meeting you. By the way, my name is Josh."

"Thanks…I'm Adam. Hey, I didn't mean to chase you off, it's just that. look, maybe we can do this again sometime."

"Yeah, maybe, I don't know."

"Right, listen, you go on and I'll throw out the table trash."

"God bless and keep you Adam, whatever you do—don't stop listening. Find your believement. It's the only thing you'll be able to take with you."

"Yeah, Josh, you just keep believing and thanks for the coffee."

CHAPTER EIGHT

There are two kinds of people: those who say to God, "Thy will be done," and those to whom God says, "All right, then, have it your way.

Quotation
C. S. Lewis
British Scholar and Novelist, 1898-1963

'It's the only ***thing you'll be able to take with you.*** *Take it with me? Take it with me where? Oh brother, now he's got me asking myself those weird questions!*

I didn't realize what time it is. Where did it go? I've got to get ready for my date tonight. Wow, they're still working on that poor guy, at least they have him off oxygen. I wonder if that's a good thing or a bad.what the.that guy...I know him, I mean I...that's not possible. That's impossible!

Got to check this out. I don't know if they'll let me talk to him or not. I'll just signal like I'm related, and maybe they'll buy it. Oh, man, please let them buy it.

"Josh? Is...is that you? How in the world—"

"How in the world...I know you?"

"Listen, this will sound crazy. We.I was just in the bookstore having coffee with you, and we were talking about the guy out in the ambulance and about the concept of god, and.how is this happening?"

"How does it matter?"

"Are you kidding me? It matters a lot! I just spent a lot of time with you and, and you just shared your entire life with me, and I spilled a lot of my guts out to you too, but I was pretty rude, and, and I was just fighting with you because it didn't matter, but.it *does* matter. You've got to believe that, you've got to live it!"

"*Believement.*"

"Yes! Yes, you remember!"

"Was...just thinking about belief. Have I lived. what I believe. *Believement.*"

"That's right, you've gotta keep on living to believe."

"I've got to keep on believing to live."

"Okay, Okay, that works too."

"Counterdoubt...faith."

Was that a ghost I was talking to in the bookstore? Is this some sort of weird dream? How could he be in the store and *in the ambulance? No, this is...real, I don't know how, but it is! What do I do? How can I help... What was that he said before?*

"Listen, Josh, the great and powerful message is really a small and very personal message, and I'm not the one who can best explain it."

"That's the only way it works."

"The only way what works? Please clon't...listen, I think I want to know more about what you have!"

"Choice...I...I believe. I'm going...to believe...to live. Do you?"

"Do I what? Do I what? Josh, please, what? Do I what? Josh! No, con't...oh, God!"

For where your treasure is, there your heart will be also.

Jesus Christ

THE BELIEVEMENT COMPANION

A Study Guide for Breaking Though
the Belief Barrier

The Believement Companion is not a manual for evangelism, but a study to help guide anyone—from the most adamant unbeliever to the most vibrant believer— through this humbling aspect of the faith walk. We all struggle at one point or another with doubt and suspicion. Sharing with one another the beautiful concept of God's grace, experiencing His forgiving character, and exposing our own remnants of unbelief are part of the adventure of helping other break through the *belief barrier*. God wants us to share the challenge with one another. The journey requires a daily commitment, seeking and submitting to God's will individually and as a community of believers in agreement. A relationship with God, walked in trust, hope and unity is all He desires and all we need. It is *believement!*

To order additional copies of *Believement: Breaking the Belief Barrier,* or to view other books written by Mark Cornelius, go to www. MarkCorneli.us or www. TatePublishing.com. and please Blog with me at www. MarkCorneli.us/blog-with-mark.

THE
BELIEVEMENT
COMPANION

A Study Guide for Breaking Though
the Belief Barrier

Mark A. Cornelius
With Foreword by Stan Toler

INTRODUCTION

The Purpose

My intentions were to create a follow-up Bible study to correlate with one of my other books ***RUT Management: Discovering Adventure in the Routine of Life***. As I dug in, I realized a good portion of my audience seemed to be cueing in on aspects of the topic I wasn't considering:

"Who says there had to be an original trailblazer—an entity before time that started the whole RUT thing?"

So my prayers changed. I started asking for understanding on the differences in perspective between God believers and God unbelievers. I began seeking clearer spiritual definition of the threshold, the *belief barrier*— where, why, how an unbeliever suddenly flips the switch and asks God into their life.

As I began the conversation, I realized, as in my own case (yes, I grew up in an unbelieving family environment), I had to put myself back in my unbeliever shoes in order to conjure the character necessary to convincingly stand firm in the face of a strong believer's testimony. Ironically, I was amazed at how difficult it was to cross back over the barrier my God had once lifted me over. The best I could do was to peer back through a very dim-looking glass, and in doing so, another irony became clear—it was the same fogged glass I had had to squint to see through from the unbeliever's side. No wonder the barrier is so difficult to break through:

What's unclear is also uninviting.

As the book developed, I confess that I hit a roadblock, even entering a discussion about Jesus Christ as Lord and Savior seems altogether a giant leap for the unbeliever. I became hesitant with the project—just where the enemy wanted me. That led to a whole lot more prayer time.

More times than not, a line of demarcation is drawn, believers and unbelievers walking to the edge of the chasm between them—only to shout an opinion across the void, hoping to make a point without building the connecting bridge of understanding and interrelationship necessary to help the unbeliever take their first steps toward a life of faith.

Believement: Breaking the Belief Barrier purposely never ties in specific biblical passages. *The Believement Companion* offers a deeper spiritual discussion, more

structured biblically related questions and scripture to validate each point the book *Believement* unveils.

My hope is that *The Believement Companion* will enable the believer not only help with self-exploration but will also enable the believer to encourage the unbeliever to make the jump over the barrier where God invites a personal and eternally deep relationship.

The Foundation

When God created man in his own image, there were no Old or New Testaments. After God convicted him, Paul did not have any New Testament writings that he carried around with him to use to convert others. The Gospel should be a simple enough and compelling enough message that the unbeliever can receive it in their own way, in their own language. Then they can explore the depth of the Word to build strength within their faith.

The Believement Companion is not designed to teach how to begin a conversation about God. It begins with the supposition that if you are a confessed Christ follower, fully devoted to a lifestyle of prayer, praise, and service, then the conversation cannot help but happen. Unbelievers, doubters, and the like will either seek your observations out of curiosity or animosity. You are, after all, obviously different.

The Believement Companion prays to be a resource of understanding as the conversation ensues. Please note that where the chapters in *Believement: Breaking Though the Barrier* are simply numbered with no titles,

The Believement Companion identifies each chapter with components critical in addressing and resolving before someone is ready to open their heart to Christ.

Warning: I, in no way, want the believer or unbeliever to think that I've come up with a magic formula for spiritual conversion. The true work is performed by a power much greater than anything known to me—a mystery that requires nothing more than a drop of faith to experience. Others can walk with the seeker to the altar, but the true moment of wonder occurs when all of these components are revealed by the Holy Spirit, only then can the seeker become a willing vessel.

God created the world as an incubator for active relationships between people.

The question is, how to explain the incredible personal relationship that is available with God Himself to someone who most likely doubts their Creator's very existence. He is invisible—therefore, He doesn't count.

As this study compelled me to reexamine an affirm my own beliefs, I pray it leads you to a lifetime of incredible witnessing opportunities.

Let your believement shine!

A Prayer to Reach Across the Barrier

Lord, You well know, the challenge You laid out for me in writing this guide was to help me see and understand the drawn line—what makes a believer a believer, and what makes an unbeliever an unbeliever? As I studied and prayed, it became clear that, as in all things, only You can draw that line and only You can inspire the leap over that barrier of belief. So my purpose in this work is only to reveal what the barrier looks like from a human perspective and what both an unbeliever and a believer would see differently when confronting the barrier. To prepare, I had to begin with the foundation of my faith.

Creator, You offer me

> *Your grace and forgiveness, planned for me before I even existed; and Your love, even to the point of sacrificing Yourself in the death of Your son—to have a relationship with me in spite of, and to take away, my imperfections.*

This foundation is the greatest of gifts that You have given me, and on it I build my faith. But Eternal, "You did not give me faith for the purpose of inaction. You have shown me that faith is to be built upon, inspiring action and growth.

So You have bestowed more gifts, four foundational posts that You have shown me:

> In the beginning was the Word, and the Word was with God, and the Word was God. He was in the beginning with God. All things were made through him, and without him was not any thing made that was made. In him was life, and the life was the light of men. The light shines in the darkness, and the darkness has not overcome it.
>
> John 1:1-5

> For God so loved the world, that he gave his only Son, that whoever believes in him should not perish but have eternal life. For God did not send his Son into the world to condemn the world, but in order that the world might be saved through him. Whoever believes in him is not condemned, but whoever does not believe is condemned already, because he has not believed in the name of the only Son of God.
>
> John 3:16-18

> Jesus said to him, "I am the way, and the truth, and the life. No one comes to the Father except through me. If you had known me, you would have known my Father also. From now on you do know him and have seen him."
>
> John 14:6-7

> Therefore, since we have been justified by faith, we have peace with God through our Lord Jesus Christ. Through

him we have also obtained access by faith into this grace in
which we stand, and we rejoice in hope of the glory of God.

Romans 5:1-2

Master, anyone walking through *The Believement Companion* will
observe these posts throughout. That's spelled T-H-E-O-L-O-G-Y. On
these posts, You have set the course of my spiritual journey. On them is
built the bridge that brings me ever closer to being what You have always
had in mind for me, to be more and more like Jesus.

I know that this is where others of faith may struggle, seeing the posts
not as a structure for growth, but as a barrier to their perception of personal
development. I know this because I struggled for years, seeing Your path as
an obstacle, instead of walking on the bridge that existed so nearby. Praise
you, Father, for patiently, lovingly encouraging me with direction, even
when I seemed reluctant to be led.

Adonai, You have also introduced me to other such people who have
claimed faith but who also struggle with breaking through the same
foundational barriers. Help me, as Psalm 19 suggests, give testimony to
Your Word, "making wise the simple."

What You have revealed is that the posts support some very specific
planks—biblical truths based on Old and New Testament scripture
without which the bridge over the barrier can't be built. To You, my God,
and to those considering walking through *The Believement Companion*
with me, I offer my *statement of faith*, the road signs that keep me focused
on my journey of *believement*.

Biblical Statement of Faith

- God is God—there is only one (Exodus 20:1, Ephesians 4:6)

- God is holy—perfect, without fault (Psalm 99.9, Revelation 4:8)
  God is eternal—He existed before anything else, including time
  (Dueteronomy 33:27, Romans 16:26)

- God is a trinity comprised of three major characteristics—

  o Father of all creation (1 Chronicles 29 Psalm 89:26,:10,1
  Corinthians 8:6)

- o Spirit that is the enabler and inspiration of life (Exodus 31:3, 1 Samuel 10:10, Matthew 3:16, Acts 1:8)
- o Son who is the appointed king of creation (Isaiah 9:6, John 1:1—5, John 10:25—30, 1 Corinthians 8:6)

- The Spirit of God actively and frequently influences lives (Isaiah 61:1, Romans 8:9)

- Jesus Christ is the only son of God—
  - o He chose to sacrifice himself in human form to save mankind from spiritual death. (Isaiah 53:1—12, John 3:16—17)
  - o The only way to have an eternal relation- ship/life with God is to accept and believe in Jesus Christ as my personal lord and savior (Isaiah 49:6—12, John 14:6)

- Mankind is not God (see point number one)

- Mankind is not holy (see point number two)

- God designed and created mankind with a free will, requiring a committed choice to—
  - o Seek God; rejecting their own will and embracing God's will or (Deuteronomy 11:13-15, Acts 5:29)
  - o Reject God's will, in preference to their own will. (Deuteronomy 11:16-17, Ephesians 2:1-3)

- Mankind is born having to make the choice of seeking God-
  - o The choice is not made for them (Proverbs 3:5-6, Proverbs 28:14, 1 Pe 2:8)
  - o Choosing one's personal desires over God's desires for them is called sin—a separation from God (Genesis 4-7, Matthew 13:40-42)

- Not making the committed choice to believe in and follow God results in spiritual death (Genesis 2:17, John 8:24)

- Mankind does not by nature seek God and requires God's Spirit to enable a change in their own spiritual makeup, so that the choice becomes a new desire (1 Chronicles 28:9, John 3:18-21, Romans 3:21-27, Ephesians 2:5-10)

- The Bible, Old and New Testaments combined, is the inspired Word of God, historically and spiritually true—without contradiction (2 Samuel 22:31, Psalm 18:30, Proverbs 30:5, John 1:1, 2 Corinthinas 4:2, 1Thessalonians 2:13)

Creator of all things, I believe, at the risk of offending some, that these theological statements imply a *conviction reality*:

- A Christian believer is defined as anyone who, by personal choice, embraces *all* of the above stated points (Proverbs 3:6, John 17:21, Romans 3:3—4)

- The unbeliever is defined as anyone who, by personal choice, does not accept one or more of the above stated points (Psalm 78—32, Hebrews 3:7-10)

- Life is a journey meant to draw me closer to God and away from unbelief (Psalm 73:1-28, Hebrews 7:18-25, Hebrews 11:16, James 4:8)

Lord, I pray for both professed Christians and for those who openly declare their unbelief that You would convict their spirits by this example. Let them encounter other believers and study together the elements of this guide to validate or eliminate their faith questions by testing them as suggested by Paul in Romans 12:1-2.

Destination Beyond the Barrier

Before walking with any seeker to help them discover the path, the actual destination the path leads to should be very well understood. This study is designed to enable believers to help unbelievers break through, crossing over the *belief barrier* separating them from an eternal relationship with God and accept Jesus Christ as Lord and Savior.

The Path to the Destination

The conversation that begins the breakdown of the *belief barrier* appears on the surface to be anything but an invitation to faith. That's because the unbeliever typically has a different starting point and objective than the believer. An unbeliever, or someone who has a faith base different from mine, wants to minimize conviction and commitment to an intellectual or social dialogue.

Each chapter in *The Believement Companion* will examine the attitudes and foundational position/ beliefs that make up the two characters in the book *Believement: Breaking Through the Belief Barrier.*

Adam, the unbeliever, supports his positions using ideas gathered from many ideas and faiths. He represents moral relativism, a concept based on the philosophy of humanism—the idea that mankind has the ability to work out its problems and is, by nature, good. By this example, mankind controls its own destiny and only needs to mature on its own, everyone putting their best ideas and behavior forward (and accepting whatever others believe in themselves to be good) to achieve eventual perfection. In this way, mankind separates itself and depends on the currents of culture and a continual battle for power by individuals and groups seeking domination.

Josh, the believer, follows the Judeo-Christian God. He represents those who depend on faith (a very difficult concept for unbelievers and believers alike to define and defend) in a Perfectly Superior Entity. God, though unseen, is active not only in the universe, desir-

ing a deep personal relationship with every individual. By this example, mankind must recognize its flaws, not its independent accomplishments, and more importantly, surrender all control to God, submitting to His order, believing that only He can forgive/salvage/per- fect the individual. In this way, God offers an eternal relationship with mankind.

Chapter titles reflect where a relationship with God begins and how it can develop. *The Believement Companion* will then lay out the arguments and questions that compel unbeliever and believer. The structure of every chapter will be the same and include eight progressive segments. Each segment will encourage personal exploration, group discussion, and will request additional input to welcome the rich and unique example that God creates through His influence in each believer.

Study Segments

The chapters of *The Believement Companion* are separated into distinct segments for study purposes. First is a summary of observations about belief and unbelief as portrayed in *Believement: Breaking Through the Belief Barrier*. Then prayer is offered, acknowledging that God is partner in this exploration. Next is the presentation of perspectives including questions from both an unbeliever's and a believer's positions.

The question section is unique in that the questions of the believer are not designed to correct or match those of the unbeliever—the believer's questions should be considered as *invitational* tools, intended to address the defensive nature of the unbeliever, challenging them to think in a more positive light about belief in God.

Then will follow supporting evidence of God's participation in the dialogue through scripture and testimony. At the end of each chapter, a confession/invita- tion is offered—the idea being that the believer should be ready to recognize their own shortcomings before being ready to invite the unbeliever over the barrier. Finally, a survey is offered that allows the individual to examine their personal walk with God, encouraging further prayer, study and reflection to strengthen their spiritual relationship.

Each study segment will be highlighted in borders for easy reference as shown on the next page. Many of the segments will ask questions and encourage responses. Because of the constraints of this book's size, make sure to have extra paper available for writing responses.. What you will get out of this exercise will only be as valuable as your own discoveries, so don't be afraid to embellish and expound!

Study Segments

Observations of Belief vs. Unbelief

Prayer

Perspective Chart

Unbeliever's Barrier Perspective	Believer's Barrier Perspective

Barrier Building Questions	Barrier Breaking Questions

Breakthrough Bible Passages

Breakthrough Bible Passages

Additional Personal Passages

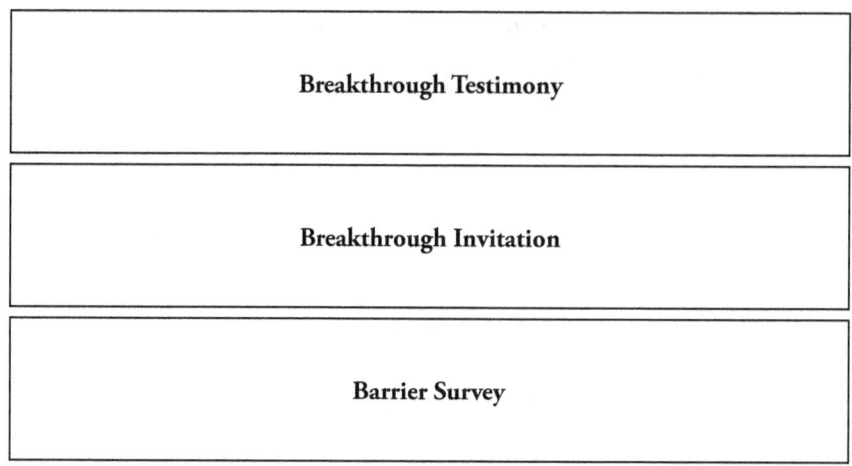

Important

It will be up to the reader (or study group) to set the pace, method, and tone for discussion. Don't rush through any part of the *Believement* story or *The Believement Companion* segments, especially if some issue confuses or convicts you. If you want to read one chapter and then go through the corresponding companion segments, great, but make sure that each participant reads *Believement: Breaking Through the Belief Barrier* prior to or in conjunction with going through this companion study.

The Compelling Reality

Oh yes, there is one more important element concerning the journey from unbelief to belief. Even Paul, one of the most dedicated and resolute believers of all time, confessed that he struggled with unbelief—as did the man who, in faith, brought his son to be healed by Jesus in Mark 9:17—24. Unbelief is not like a skin totally shed when belief in God and Jesus is confessed. It is instead a compass point, turned away from. I as an individual still turn back and am tempted to head in the direction of my unbelief—sometimes the *back-sliding* is a brief journey, sometimes a struggled trek. The confusion only ends when I focus my attention on my intended and desired destination, when I turn and peer in the right direction, toward becoming more and more like my Savior—until He says, the journey is complete.

SEPARATION

People might think that before there is belief in God, there is no relationship with God, but in this most unique of all relationships, it is just the opposite. God loves all people, desperately wanting love in return from each individual. I can't, no one can, grasp the depth of that kind of love. But once I placed my faith in the fact that such a love existed, the invisible became visible. More than that, it became sharper and clearer than any other part of reality, suggesting it was the foundation of all things.

An unbeliever on the other side of the *belief barrier* who hasn't experienced this animation of reality doesn't have the advantage or confidence it gives to the broken-through believer. Where the believer is certain God exists, the unbeliever may be as strongly convinced that there is no spiritual presence outside of themselves, or that any spiritual presence that does exist is not interested in them. Unbelievers typically understand faith and relationship as human qualities, not godly creations.

So when sharing faith with another individual, establish a bond. Seek common concerns and needs before expecting anyone to listen to and respect your passion for God and His Word. Ask yourself how you would justify your commitment of belief to another person who is equally unbelieving? How would you encourage continued dialogue to develop a relationship with such a person?

Prayer

I see and hear people all the time either complaining about the conditions around them or pointing a finger at the very one who can help heal the problems—they seem to be offended by You, Lord, without even thinking You really exist, instead focusing their distaste, even hatred on those who choose to follow You.

Father, I know we too were once separated. I know who caused that to happen, and I am so sorry—draw near to me. Lord, I pray that You help me when I speak to those who still do not know you. Let my language be their language, but spoken with Your heart. Help me to love them as You love them. Help me to listen and respond with Your Spirit filling and guiding my actions.

Perspective Comparison

Just because you believe or don't believe in God doesn't mean that your view of life is totally stable. You may often find yourself being drawn toward the other side—whichever other side that may be for you. The awareness of what attracts you there is important. Compare and discuss with others the perspectives listed on both sides of Perspective Chart I. Add additional comparisons that you believe distinguish the believer from the unbeliever. Consider your own perspective and honestly assess which of the listed traits describes you. Then write answers to the questions below:

Ask— "Am I who I want to be? Why, why not?

If the answer is no, then— "What must I do to change?"

If the answer is yes, then— "What must I do to encourage others to explore their belief and to challenge their unbelief?"

Perspective Chart I

Unbeliever's Barrier Perspective	Believer's Barrier Perspective
Distrustful of the concept that a god exists	Trusting in God's active role in the world
Typically skeptical when conversation begins	Typically anxious to share personal experience of their own walk with God
Wanting immediate answers to satisfy their curiosity, not to challenge their current beliefs	Tend to answer questions with more questions or rephrase questions to point out contradictions in belief or lifestyle
Becomes defensive when confronted with spiritual truth that contradicts their current beliefs	Sometimes respond to defensiveness by backing off of positions of personal belief, or by holding on to and stating a position so firmly that the Unbeliever perceives the believer to be intractable and stops receiving.

Barrier Building Questions	Barrier Breaking Questions
What gives you the right, privilege, or authority to tell me what is right?	Can I share a personal experience with you?
Why is belief in a higher spiritual power important at all?	Do you believe in a higher spiritual power?
How does your life experience relate to my life experience?	Have you ever had a crisis in your life or watched others in crisis and wondered- if there is a God, why doesn't he help?
How can you possibly believe that you are right in your understanding of the existence of God?	Can you tell me about your experience with faith and what you've found to be true about God?
Doesn't mankind have the ability to fix its own problems without outside help?	Tell me about what problems you think mankind has permanently fixed over the course of time?
Why do religions use fear as a motivator?	Define what you believe fear is?
Don't I have the right to chose if I believe in god, or what I believe god to be?	What prevents you from living every single moment trying to seek out ways to love God?

Breakthrough Bible Passages

Gen 3:1-7, Exo 14:10-12, Deu 28:58-68, Job 22:12-17, 2, Mat 13::47-50, Rom 8:5-8, Cor 3:14-18, Jas 4

Read the passages above; then write in additional personal passages that speak to you personally about the conflict between spiritual belief and unbelief in each individual.

Additional Personal Passages

Pick out at least one passage from the Breakthrough Bible Passages above, and one of your Additional Personal Passages. Read the entire Bible chapter or section where the passages are embedded to understand their context. Explain how each speaks to your understanding of the barrier between belief and unbelief:

Breakthrough Testimony

Pray about the passages above and then write out your story of how you overcame unbelief and fear to recognize God's power over your life and how this led to your accepting Jesus Christ as your Lord and Savior. Include the personal challenges and blessings that your choice to follow Jesus now provokes in your daily life:

Breakthrough Invitation

Lord Jesus, I look back, trying to remember how different my life was before fully accepting You as my Savior and Lord. Thank You for healing my spirit so fully— reconnecting my spirit to Your Spirit. So that now, my past life has become foggy and difficult to remember— as I continue to draw closer to you. But, Lord, I know someone else that I want to walk with on their path to discovering Your love. I know it's You who calls out to their spirit across the barrier. I know I am not the one who leads them over the divide. I know that I can only walk with them to the altar of their heart, and that they must meet You, accept and follow You of their own choice. Help me to be patient and open to their questions, wise and Spirit-filled in my responses. Help them to be inquisitive and receptive to Your desires. Help me and them to discover together Your calling for our lives beyond separation.

Barrier Survey	
Strong Unbelief	Strong Belief

Mark where you fall on this scale. Justify your perception of the strength of your unbelief or belief (or your non-commitment to either). If you are totally committed one way or the other, explain how you came to that position. If you fall anywhere in between, explain what holds you back from total commitment.

Character

"Who desires relationship?" Most people would easily answer this question with "I do." But when asked, "What are you willing to commit to in order to make a relationship last?" the answer usually is very conditional with expectations being more focused on what we expect the other party of the relationship to do and how we expect them to behave to please us.

Even in my expectations of a relationship with God, it seems more emphasis is placed on what He will provide me rather than what I bring to the relationship.

God desires relationship, just as we do. He created us for a relationship with Him, but how does His character differ from ours, what are His expectations, and what is His view of who we are? Are we compatible with God? What needs to happen to make us willing to be changed in preparation for the most extraordinary of relationships?

Prayer

Father of the Universe, I had a starting point in time when I was able to begin perceiving the world around me—the physical. Later I began to perceive the things unseen around me—the spiritual. But my perceptions were, and are, shortsighted, my understanding limited, therefore my behavior, even my character, is in need of refinement.

Master, Your character is perfect, holy, without limit. You existed before anyone, anything. You have never not existed. It's difficult for me to comprehend this fact and to acknowledge the depths of Your wisdom, Your prescience and involvement in all things. And I am a believer.

I look back to my unbelief and the even greater limits that blinded me. I not only didn't know of Your infinite majesty; I didn't really care. I pretended, but I didn't pursue. I was vague in my curiosity, but not convicted to search out the truth of Your character.

So, Lord, I confess, I was unwilling to recognize how much greater than me You are. I wanted to think I too had power and that my power was somehow growing, and that someday, my power would be great. I also confess that some days, I slip back into that pattern of thinking—that I am a good controller of my corner of my world.

Why would You love someone like me? It is the greatest of unanswered questions, yet some don't even bother to ask for, or desire, Your love—not even seeing Your love at work around them. Help us not only see Your desire for relationship but also long to embrace it. Let it invade us without question. Let Your love change us, not into creatures of our own ambitions, but into vessels of Your possibilities, pouring out Your blessings through us to others in need.

Perspective Comparison

When you step back to look at your relationship with God, does it seem complete? Is it personal and intimate, or distant and formal? Do you perceive God as living with you 24/7 or as a visitor to your existence? Compare and discuss with others the perspectives listed on both sides of Perspective Chart II. Add additional comparisons that you believe distinguish the believer from the unbeliever. Consider your own perspective and honestly assess which of the listed traits describes you. Then write answers to the questions below:

Ask— "Is my current relationship with God the one He desires for us? Why, why not?

If the answer is no, then— "What must I do to change?"

If the answer is yes, then— What must I do to encourage others to deepen their relationship with God?"

Perspective Chart II

Believer's Barrier Perspective	Unbeliever's Barrier Perspective
Have difficulty explaining how they are imperfect in their day to day behavior, but perfected by Christ in their spiritual being.	Reluctant to take the spiritual conversation to the "next level" that a requires a sharing of personal faults and failed attempts.
Have trouble explaining holiness as a character trait, instead focusing 1 on what mankind is 'not'— giving the impression of being judgmental and pious	Seldom try to understand how the trait of holiness in God, also defines a the great separator between God and o mankind— unholiness.
Struggle to explain how God completes us in Christ and relates to us through His Spirit.	Fail to connect the reasoning that God i complete, while we are incomplete to the truth that God, c being perfect, could not directly interact with imperfection.
Jump ahead of the problem- they seem anxious to explain to someone who fails to recognize that they are e bleeding to death that there is a doctor who has made the need for blood totally unnecessary.	Miss the significance of Jesus' willingness to become human, die and resurrect on our behalf; to remake b us perfect in His image— that we d can then have a perfect relationship through Him with God.
More concerned with how God d defines the individual	The unbeliever focuses on defining God
Have difficulty describing the desire for relationship of God to humankind— why would someone holy want to create and associate with the unholy? (The Acceptance Paradox)	Can't define the similarities between God and humankind because of the reluctance to acknowledge the differences between God and humankind (The Denial Paradox)
Define God as: • ALL powerful • Capable of unlimited action to influence humankind • Loving His creation a • Interactive with people on a personal level • Reaching out to humanity; even becoming human by predetermined action as a solution to a manmade problem	Define God (if believed He even exists) as: • Only partially powerful • Capable of only limited action to influence humankind • Not loving His creation • Not interactive with people on a personal level • Not reaching out to humanity or becoming human by predetermined action as a solution to a manmade problem

Barrier Building Questions	Barrier Breaking Questions
How can you expect me to comprehend something I can't see?	What traits would you want to see God exhibit?
Why even bother to explore what god is?	If there is a Supreme Being greater than any other thing that exists, should that Being be the main focus of our attention?
Who, besides god (if there is one), has the right to define god?	Do we define God or does God define us?
If no religion or person has correctly defined man's relationship to god, how would someone know if they've discovered god?	Have you ever prayed, believing there is someone actually listening?
If there is a god, who said he actually cares what happens to us?	What evidence do you have that God doesn't care what happens to us?
If god does care, why doesn't he fix the world?	How would you have God fix the world?
If god cares for me personally, wouldn't he answer when I call out to him?	Does God have to answer you with the answer you want in order to be God?
Why is your god undependable?	Do you depend on God for everything?
Why is your god inconsistent?	
If your god is so great and loving, why do bad things happen?	Are you willing to study closely just how consistent God is?
If there is a god, why did he create such a bad world?	Tell me about the bad things that have happened to you?
Why would god even want to bother with creating something that he knew would go wrong?	Why is the world bad?
	What do you think would make such a creation desirable to God?
How would someone be able to figure out all of what this god of yours is?	Is your perception of who God is growing as you study about Him?

Breakthrough Bible Passages

Gen 24:27, Gen 32:10, Exo 15:2-13, Exo 20:5, Exo 33:1920, Exo 34:6-7, Num 14:18, Deu 3:27, Deu 7:7-10, Psa 7:811, Psa 29:4, Psa 78:59, Psa 104:24, Psa 104:30, Isa 9:6-7, Isa 51:21-23, Isa 52:5-7, Mat 11:27-30, Luk 10:21-22, Luk 18:24, Joh 10:25-30, Joh 11:35, Rom 1:18, Rom 2:5, Rom 12:19, Rom 15:13, Rom 16:20, Rom 16:25-27, 1 Cor 14:33, 2 Cor 13:11, Eph 1:3-12, Eph 2:4-8, 1 Th 5:23, Tit 3:3-7, Heb, 1:1-4, Heb 4:12, Heb 6:13-18, 1 Pe 3:18-20

Read the passages above; then write in additional personal passages that speak to you personally about how the character of God compares to the character of mankind.

Additional Personal Passages

Pick out at least one passage from the Breakthrough Bible Passages above, and one of your Additional Personal Passages. Read the entire Bible chapter or section where the passages are embedded to understand their context. Explain how each speaks to your understanding of God's character compared to a believer's character and to the character of an unbeliever:

Breakthrough Testimony

Pray about the passages above and then write out your story of how you are striving to become more like Jesus in character and spirit. Include the personal challenges and blessings this now provokes in your daily life:

Breakthrough Invitation

Creator of all things, I am the creator of nothing. What I do of my own will destroy what You have so perfectly set in motion. Why can't I see and recognize at the time I attempt to set my own plans in motion that You are there, saddened by the attempt, longing for me to look in Your direction, eager for me to seek Christ within me and follow his example.

For that to happen, wouldn't I have to be different somehow? After all, You're different from me—spir- itual, perfect in every way. What would I have to do? What would I have to become? How would I have to be enabled to see You, to hear You? How would I even be able to recognize You?

Lord, I believe, but it's my unbelief that still tempts me to ignore You, to be different from You. Help me be tuned into the struggle I once had as a total unbeliever who didn't recognize you at all, who tried to justify my actions and opinions as necessary for living in a senseless world. Let that memory serve me in witnessing to others, of how You can open the eyes of anyone willing, to experience an incredible new world in which You dwell with us.

Barrier Survey

Unbeliever Characteristics	Believer Characteristics

In each box above, write a list of characteristics that you think uniquely belong to the unbeliever and those that identify the believer. Once completed, answer this question: What must I understand about the character of God and the character of humankind so that I can be prepared for a conversation with an unbeliever about the differences and the commonalities between God and humankind?

CHOICE

Where did it all start? No, not the question of our origin, the most puzzling of questions is, When did we first start questioning? Not that questioning is a bad thing, but my curiosity about the world and the things around me invites another seemingly harmless, normal, yet deeply diabolical question.

"What do I choose?"

We ask the choice' question countless ways such as the following:

- Which way do I turn?
- Who is better for me to like or love?
- Is this good or bad for me?

The choice is not in what to do, but whom am I doing it for? So how do I know the difference between what God wants and what I want? It's seldom clear.

I've learned (and have to be constantly reminded of the lesson) that faith in God requires not trusting my questions of choice, but choosing His answers of trust. I've had to learn to listen in a whole new way, through biblical study, listening to and watching the lives of strong believers whom I've surrounded myself with. And I've discovered this way; my questions of direction and purpose have already been answered for me. Suddenly, there is no choice, only a question, the most controversial and confrontational of all questions:

What do You want me to do, God?

The *trust question*, some argue, is ridiculous when put to the extreme test. Strict unbelievers accuse, "You mean you'd sit at a stoplight and ask your god whether he wants you to turn or go straight? How do you accomplish anything?"

They have a point. Responding to the *trust question* can get dangerous! Holy Jihad and crusades have been waged based on misinterpretation of the *trust question*. The temptation is to rationalize any action, saying, "I'm going to do this for God." We've all done it—justified our desires by claiming them to be marching orders from the Almighty.

The argument on both sides is a sinister distraction causing believers and unbelievers alike to miss the point—God's will is not hard to see in action. The model is found biblically in Jesus, and day to day in the example of those who seek to be like him. Do those people actually exist? Sadly, there don't appear to be many, but you can't mistake them when you find one. They are the ones walking out their lives in love and total confidence that God will guide them, no matter what choices might tempt them away from the clear purpose God has put before them, because they dare to live every moment of every day with the *trust question* as their compass held out before them to point the way.

After all, if you know only one direction is the right direction, the choice is no choice at all!

Prayer

Adonai, some things look good to me, some things I recognize as bad, and on these measurements, through my eyes, I've made and continue to make many decisions. This is dry, good for sleeping on; this is soggy, stay away; this I want; this I don't want; what I want is good; what I don't want is bad...

And suddenly, Lord, I've forgotten what it was like not to have to choose, not to have to judge, not to have to discern. I've forgotten how You cared for me so that I could care only about You, Lord.

I've struggled with this, because at one time, I didn't believe in the existence of such a place as a perfect garden on earth, where first man, second man, any man. where I could physically walk and talk with You. What a fairy tale it seems.

And that's exactly as it should seem. I can't be in that place, can I? Those who deny Your existence, deny the place's existence. Even many who claim You as God over their lives think of the garden in past tense and/

or a future, far, far away, just as they perceive You to be a God of past and future only, far, far away from the present.

But what if that's not the case? What if this is misperception—part of the knowledge paradox (I can't see it because I don't trust it—I don't trust it because I can't see it) we have chosen for ourselves?

My daughter and I had a recent walk together in our special private garden place, Lord. We were talking about the tree of the knowledge of good and evil. She's so profoundly aware of You—thank You for that. I asked her what she thought of the idea that, by eating of the fruit of that tree in the garden of Eden, we suddenly became aware of what was both good and what was bad, not just one or the other. Her response was beautiful. "Well, duh! God didn't say to not eat one fruit, or the other, from that tree—there was only one kind of fruit not to choose."

It was a command You gave—*don't eat*—not a request. My daughter gets that, Lord. I get it. The puzzle is, why do we want it to be a choice?

Perspective Comparison

Try to think back to the moment you chose to accept Jesus Christ as Lord and Savior. Did you realize the gravity of the commitment? Were you thinking of how the choice you were about to make would affect all your decisions from that point forward? Did you perceive God's interaction in helping you with your choice? Did it change how you acted and made decisions in your day to day, moment to moment, from that point forward? Compare and discuss with others the perspectives listed on both sides of

Perspective Chart III. Add additional comparisons that you believe distinguish how a believer makes decisions from the decision making process of an unbeliever. Consider your own perspective and honestly assess which of the listed traits describes you. Then write answers to the questions below:

Ask— "Am I who God chooses me to be? Why, why not?"

If the answer is no, then— "What must I do to change?"

If the answer is yes, then— "What must I do to encourage others in their choices of belief versus unbelief?"

Perspective Chart III

Unbeliever's Barrier Perspective	Believer's Barrier Perspective
Choosing is good, even Christians talk about free will being a part of the human condition.	There is only one choice to make— believe in Jesus Christ as my Lord and Savior. All other actions are responses to that calling
If I make good choices I'm a good person; if I make bad choices I need to try harder.	My good or bad choices do not make me anything. I am incomplete without Christ and, if I focus only on following Christ and His word, I'm freed from the judgement of my choices.
If there is no god, whatever choices I make are judged strictly on the merit of the outcome based those choices	
If there is a god, whatever choices I make are judged on my intent to do good or bad	Tend to point out the obvious— that humans cannot please God unless they simply submit to God's will— to unbelievers who don't comprehend or rebel against the idea that they are not in control
Place little or no value on a god's concern that people follow his will	God doesn't merit my actions based on my good or bad intent, but on my willingness to search out His will and submit to its direction
	Wrestle with accepting the gifts mercy and grace, sometimes becoming too concerned as to whether or not God will be pleased with the outcomes of a faithful lifestyle instead of focusing on the intent of a faithful lifestyle.

Barrier Breaking Questions	Barrier Building Questions
What's wrong with the concept of people having the right to choose, to be free; to not have someone else telling them how to think?	So the disagreements and struggles you see going on around you may have nothing to do with God, but instead with your desire to be the 'chooser' of outcomes instead of God?
What's the big rush in making a choice to believe or not believe in God? Isn't that a personal decision that should be done carefully and thoughtfully?	Help me understand, by your example, what careful steps should be taken and how someone should thoughtfully make the decision to or not to believe in God?
If there was a god, wouldn't he have stopped all the bad choices from happening?	What if there used to be, and still could be, a way of living where noone fought, there was no disease; no spiritual, mental or physical disruption of any kind?
What if I chose NOT to love a god? In your god-world, what happens?	If God is truly God and not a man-made fantasy, why would someone not love Him?
Are you happy with the idea of someone else making your choices for you and not allowing you any freedom to be creative in your choices?	Are you satisfied with allowing others besides God or yourself, people you don't even know or trust make choices that affect your life?
Can't I make my own choices and then ask your god to help me make them work out Okay? Isn't that what prayer is about?	What if the only choice you ever had to make was that of believing in God?
What if your god chose not to love us-just decided to go live in another part of the universe- leaving us here on our own?	Do you ever long to see or hear God? Where does that longing start? Why was it created in you?
Do you really believe that your god will make every decision for you- "make a left turn here, a right there, pull in at the next rest stop"- isn't that naive?	When you are not sure what to do and hear someone whom you really respect say, "trust me, I know how to help you", do you trust them or look for another option?

Breakthrough Bible Passages

Exo 13:21-22, Deu 12:8-12, Deu 23:14-16, Deu 30:9-20, Jos 24:15, Psa 25:12-14, Pro 1:23-33, Pro 3:5-6, Psa 25:46, Psa 43:3, Pro 8:6-20, Neh 9:18-20, Isa 42:16, Isa 49:810, Jer 2:17-21, Mat 24:11, Luk 9:22-25, Luk 14:7-11, Joh 10:25-30, Joh 15:16, Joh 12:24-26, 1 Cor 1:27-31, 1 Cor 7:17

Read the passages above; then write in additional personal passages that speak to you personally about the choices you make and those you see being made by others.

Additional Personal Passages

Pick out at least one passage from the Breakthrough Bible Passages above, and one of your Additional Personal Passages. Read the entire Bible chapter or section where the passages are embedded to understand their context. Explain how each speaks to your understanding of God's idea of choice compared to a believer's choices and to the choices of an unbeliever:

Breakthrough Testimony

Pray about the passages above and then write out your story of how your choices and the decisions you've made, both before and after accepting Jesus as your Lord and Savior, have affected you. Include the personal challenges and blessings this now provokes in your daily life and in the lives of those around you:

Breakthrough Invitation

My stupidity has provided me with a tool. I now comprehend what I didn't before. What if such a place as the garden of Eden actually exists here and now? Master, can I walk with You right here, right now? On earth as it is in heaven? Oh, my God, what if that were a real possibility? What if I'm not sure You exist—even deny You exist, but the possibility of You being a personal God is a reality? What would that mean to me, and why don't You just tap me on the shoulder (gently please) to prove Your existence to me?

I want to do the thinking and the deciding, then have You fix the consequences—it's the conundrum not of free will, but of desiring the knowledge of good and evil, wanting control over either or both is the problem, and now I'm on a path parallel to the one my Master intended. The garden isn't far away in some special land hidden by a science fiction cloaking device. It's always close by, always just to my west, always just out of reach, but the combination to the security gate that would admit me back in has never changed.

Lord, I want to submit to You, be obedient to You, love and follow You before all things. Lead me back to the garden. Be my source, my companion, and my destination.

Barrier Survey

Unbeliever Commitment	Believer Commitment

In each box above, write things an unbeliever is committed to, verses those things a believer is committed to. Once completed, answer this question: What is involved in loving God totally, twenty-four/seven; totally trusting that He'll provide me with everything I need? How does my unbelief interfere with my choice to love God?

UNBELIEF

ápistos [faithless, unbelieving], apisteo [to disbelieve, be unfaithful], apistfa [unfaithfulness, unbelief]—Greek.

In *BELIEVEMENT: BREAKING through the Belief Barrier*, Adam doesn't see enough proof that God exists. Or so he claims. When confronted with any evidence whatsoever of God's active participation in world and personal events, those who say they don't believe in God often appear to become agitated. They seem offended by the very attempt to seek God out.

Could it be that some people actually fear the potential of the existence of God—content that no matter how bad or crazy life may get in a godless world, it would be that much worse in a world created by a supreme being? Could it be that they fear such a world would require a commitment they're just not ready to make? So by claiming God doesn't exist, neither does the need for the worship commitment. The choice of no choice: why bother exploring your origin if part of that discovery causes you to have to shift from a position you're dead set on keeping?

Christians, Jews, Muslims view their world as constructed by a supreme being. Other Eastern, Asian, and even Native American cultures look at nature as its own energy force possessed of personality traits—Ghia, Mother Nature, et cetera—that interact in mysterious ways with the physical world.

Compare this with human relativism whereby any faith is Okay. As a matter of fact, all faith is Okay. Don't dare suggest that your faith is better than my faith. If you do, your faith becomes forfeit. In other words, strong faith that suggests a higher purpose than another faith negates *all* faiths— they can't coexist, so at the end of the argument, *none* exist.

So many choices and *unchoices*, how can I chose?

Prayer

I am a doubter, I'm suspicious, I don't trust…where did these traits come from, Lord? They are not Yours. You have belief, You have faith, You trust. And You have offered these gifts to me as well.

And this admission coming from a believer! What about the unbeliever who even doubts Your existence, who can't see You at work, who can't sense Your Spirit, Your closeness? How convenient I remember it being— my world was my issue to face, no one else's. If I wanted to do something, take something, be something, I simply did. Consequences? Oh yes, there were.and are.

Long-lasting consequences—some so unforeseen that they will affect me and others for life.

I thought then, Lord, that having that control, doubting You out of existence, was a good thing. But I was not considering the poor choices, the selfish deeds, the things left undone. I was only a partial god, making partial choices with permanent ramifications that I was not willing to accept as my responsibility…my fault.

Lord, I am still trying, but my trust is still weak. My belief is challenged by my unbelief, and so my obedience waivers. How can I help a complete unbeliever with the true nature of their doubt—not just that they doubt, but why they actually doubt—unless I first explore and understand my own doubt? Help me, Master, not only with my belief, but with my unbelief.

Perspective Comparison

Just because you believe or don't believe in God doesn't mean that your view of life is totally stable. You may often find yourself being drawn to the other side and the awareness of what attracts you there is important. Compare and discuss with others the perspectives listed on both sides of Perspective Chart IV. Add additional comparisons that you believe distinguish the believer from the unbeliever. Consider your own perspective and honestly assess which of the listed traits describes you. Then write answers to the questions below:

Ask— "Are there issues and circumstances in my life that I try to hide from God? Where I prefer not inviting God to walk with me? If so, what are they?"

If the answer is yes, then— "What must I do to confront my unfaithfulness and invite God's personal involvement in my life circumstances?"

If the answer is no, then— "What must I do to be sensitive to others' reluctance to invite God's personal involvement in their life circumstances?"

Unbeliever's Barrier Perspective	Believer's Barrier Perspective
Doubtful of God's existence and therefore confused and conflicted as to what forces control their life.	Trusting in God's existence, but sometimes doubtful of God's direct interaction in their life
Looks for ways to disprove the divine power over them	Looks for ways to validate the divine power over them
Embraces logical or physical explanation that others offer to explain the condition of the world and humankind including the 'unexplainable and the chaotic'	Looks to faith in God for explanations to the 'unexplainable and the chaotic'. But has difficulty communicating the concept faith to unbelievers
Continues through life to investigate alternative explanations for the unexplainable and the chaotic' but seldom resolve contradictions, embracing what fits best with their self interests	When practicing faith, discover that it becomes easier over time to see God at work in them and around them, alienating them even further in lifestyle, language and spiritual opinions from unbelievers
Dismiss Biblical explanations as archaic, inconsistent and contradictory, citing single passages and stories, seldom researching deeply to connect all a aspects of the Biblical perspective.	Begin to search out Biblical explanations and learn to cross reference—discovering deeper meanings and validation of Biblical accuracy
Tend to blame others for tragedy Go and bad things happening in the world, or dismiss them as the 'nature of things'	Tend to be self blaming, looking to God for redemption
Point toward disaster and tragedy as proof that God doesn't exist	Pray for self and others needs in good and bad circumstances, looking to God for remedy

Barrier Building Questions	Barrier Breaking Questions
Why do you believe in a god that you can't see?	Do you ever suspect that something is going on "behind the scenes of life?
Tell me what proof there is that a god exists?	Do you really want to believe in God, or are you seeking to prove that He doesn't exist?
What's wrong with believing in Evolution?	Explain to me how something is created from nothing?
Couldn't there be natural explanations for how we all got here?	What natural proof do you need that God exists?

Breakthrough Bible Passages

Num 32:14-15, 1Sa 12:15, 2Ch 29:6, Deu 28:15-20, Neh 1:5-9, Job: 813-22, Psa 73:21-22, Ezr 9:7, Jer 17-13, Mat 13:58, Mat 14:23-32, Mar 6:6, Mar 9:24, Mar 16:14, Joh 5:37-44, Act 19:9, Rom 11:20, Rom 11:23, 1Th 1:5-10, 1Ti 1:13, Tit 1:15-16, Heb 3:19, Jud 1:3-5

Read the passages above; then write in additional personal passages that speak to you personally about the struggle you observe concerning unbelief in the world today, including how it affects your life.

Additional Personal Passages

Pick out at least one passage from the Breakthrough Bible Passages above, and one of your Additional Personal Passages. Read the entire Bible chapter or section where the passages are embedded to understand their context. Explain how each speaks to your understanding of God's existence and how the passages help you when confronting unbelief within yourself and others:

Breakthrough Testimony

Pray about the passages above and then write out your story of your unbelief and how it affects your relationship with God now. Include the personal challenges and blessings this now provokes in your daily life and in the lives of those around you:

Breakthrough Invitation

Between my unbelief and my belief, the foundation of my questions changes from "What if God doesn't exist" to "What if God does exist?"

I try, Jesus. I long to fully embrace my belief in You, but there is something within me that seeks the other explanation or that secretly hopes my actions won't be seen by You, that my selfish desires won't be discovered by You, my closest companion.

Is that it, Adonai? I do *not* doubt You! It's that, many times, I still want control, and in that wanting, I try to push You away, if but for a moment, so I can do my bidding.

I ask You, my God, to walk with me, even when I try to push You away or hide from You. Be visible to me even when I want to be invisible to You.

Barrier Survey

Unbelievers Outside the Church	Unbelievers Inside the Church

In each box above, write your observation of people outside the church and inside the church. Below, describe the difference you see in the unbelief of each. How does the unbelief of each affect their relationship with other people and with God

BELIEF

pisteuō [to believe, trust], *pistis* [faith, trust], *pistos* [faithful, trusting],*pistoō* [to make someone trust], *oligopistos* [of little faith], *oligopistia* [littleness of faith]—Greek.

Jesus frequently uses a Greek term that defines his followers in less than flattering terms. *Oligopistos* ("O you of little faith") paints a picture of a very unsure and uncertain individual, someone whose confidence in what they believe is easily distracted from God's purpose for them and from living out strong belief as a testimony for others. Why would God send His son to earth to associate with and even encourage these types of believers? Wouldn't He want the most rock solid of individuals to be His workers in the world?

The call to accept Christ as Savior should be an invitation rather than an obligation. Yes, (sadly) there has been great misinterpretation and abuse, making theChristian call to worship appear, in many instances, to be indistinguishable from other mandatory religious calls where the individual is compelled by the pressures and beliefs of others. In these sects, there is no choice but to believe, or one's physical life and social status, not just their spiritual inheritance, is immediately lowered or snuffed out completely.

So there is an evident advantage by inviting the weak believer into God's kingdom. When the weak choose God, they set themselves apart, revealing a deeper part of themselves to be nurtured and refined. They become, by their choice, more than what is expected, more than the wrestling of their belief and their unbelief—they begin to grow beyond their doubts and faults because of God's belief in them.

The Bible is very specific on the spiritual heart—the free and willing recognition of God's existence, and the acceptance of Jesus as Lord, can't be forced. Moses had to learn who God was through a personal encounter. Until confronted with a simple question from Jesus, "Why do you persecute me?" Paul refused to recognize his Messiah. He wasn't forced to accept Christ, but the reality of what he'd refused to see all along made the choice to follow…no choice at all—it became Paul's all consuming desire.

And that's the double edged sword we carry with us into any discussion with an unbeliever. How to witness without forcing our faith onto another? Here's the trick: *Oligopistos* works both ways. Just as we sometimes suffer from wavering hearts, so does even the strongest of unbelievers! So when discussing your belief with another—your job is not to make your faith someone else's, but to search for the keys that will unlock the unwilling heart. From there on, the Spirit will work. All you need to do is watch the miracle of belief unfold in their hearts and in yours.

Prayer

Savior of the **world… Savior of me^I believe. I believe You are the one true God, holy, without fault, perfect and infinite. I believe You wanted, before any other wanted; to create a Love relationship so different as to redefine Love—where there was a choice to Love, not a requirement. I believe You created me to be Loved, but that I have decided to compare You to other choices, rather than Love You without question—it is the nature of who I first chose to be— faulty. unholy.not worthy of Your offer of Love. I believe that when I made that first choice, I was dead spiritually.**

And I believe Your Love is so revolutionary, that I am Loved by You in spite of my choice. I believe that You created another way, a strange and wonderful way for me, *the unholy*, to become spiritually alive— to dwell with You, the holy. I believe You came to the world in

human form, as Jesus Christ, a man—yet still holy. I believe You lived with us and died physi-cally for us. I believe in this way, You battled death for us…for me…and won—rising from the dead, killing the unholiness—with Your death—in those of us who choose to believe in You and follow You as You have asked to be followed.

I believe You are with me now in spirit, and that my spirit— because I choose Your Love—will live forever with You. I cannot fully understand this, but I can believe it, letting it shape who I am in this world. I believe that I have a choice each day to believe this or to doubt this, but that it is true regardless of my belief. I believe that my choice now is, each day, to passionately Love You by praying with, listening, and responding to Your Spirit that lives within me. I believe that I may still wrestle with doubt. I believe I will still at times, disobey Your desire for me to be more like Your example for me—Jesus. Forgive me and help me in those times to reject my desires and replace them with Yours.

I believe I am to share these beliefs with others— in my words and my actions—loving them as You love me, without apology for what I believe, with a desire to share my love with them.teaching them to love.perfectly.

I pray, Lord, that You continue to shape me— guiding, teaching, and loving me in the way You would have me live out my belief.

Perspective Comparison

The Believement Companion starts with an outline of certain beliefs that I think crucial for the follower of Christ to recognize. But then again, my thoughts may be different from your thoughts. And our thoughts compared to those of the unbeliever?

Review the *Biblical Statement of Faith* in the introduction. Discuss the statement with others you consider to have strong faith. Compare it with the perspectives listed on both sides of Perspective Chart V. Add additional comparisons that you believe distinguish the believer's faith from the unbeliever's weakness of faith. Then write answers to the questions below:

Ask— "Do I agree with and accept all the statements listed in this *Statement of Faith?*"

If the answer is no, then— "On what biblical foundations have I built my faith? What would I add, and what do I not agree with? What specific Bible references do I use to justify my position of faith?"

If the answer is yes, then- "What beliefs and issues do I observe in others who have not crossed the barrier, and how can I best help them see how those things are distracting them from committing to a relationship with God?"

Perspective Chart V

Unbeliever's Barrier Perspective	Believer's Barrier Perspective
Wanting firm, physical evidence that a god and things spiritual exist	Dedicated without needing absolute proof (physical evidence) of God's existence and His interaction with people
Often confuse faith with superstition	
Are usually suspicious of 'believer language' that mentions a spiritual encounter experienced by another person	May struggle in identifying and 'letting go' of old beliefs, passed on by family or others, that conflict with Biblical truth
Typically defensive when their faith in other 'unseen' elements of life is pointed out	Often make statements of faith based on tradition and personal experience without having solid Biblical references to back them up
	Typically have difficulty explaining the concept of 'Only my faith in Christ and His grace saves me' to an unbeliever who doesn't recognize Jesus as God.
Barrier Building Questions	**Barrier Breaking Questions**
Why do I have to believe in your god?	Do you believe in something spiritual- some perceived "connection" between the visible and the invisible essence of the universe?
Why are all the miracles in the Bible? Why aren't miracles happening now to help me believe by seeing your god in action?	
	Tell me about a time in you're life when you couldn't explain why or how something happened to you.
Why isn't there evidence of your god that will help me believe?	
	What is the difference between unbelief and doubt?

Breakthrough Bible Passages

Deu 4:29-31, Deu 26:16-19, Deu 28:1-14, 1Sa 12:14, Isa 43:10-12, Mat 15:28, Act 6:7, Act 11:24, 1Ti 3:13, Heb 11:6

Mt. 6:30, 8:26, 14:31, 16:8, and Luke 12:28 reference oligopistis (little faith, better translated "weakened faith"). The verses and chapters in which these are found reveal insight into our worry, fear, and doubt.

Read the passages above; then write in additional personal passages that speak to you personally about the struggle you observe concerning unbelief in the world today, including how it affects your life.

Additional Personal Passages

Pick out at least one passage from the Breakthrough Bible Passages above, and one of your Additional Personal Passages. Read the entire Bible chapter or section where the passages are embedded to understand their context. Explain how each speaks to your understanding of God's existence and how the passages help you when confronting unbelief within yourself and others:

Breakthrough Bible Passages

Deu 13:1-4, Deu 23:14, Deu 30:15-20, 2Ch 30:8-9, Job 28:28, Mat 6:30, Mat 8:26, Mat 10:32-35, Mat 14:31, Mat 16:8, Mat 17:20, Mat 26:75, Luk 12:28, Jas 4:7

Read the passages above; then write in additional personal passages that speak to you personally about why you think some people have more difficulty breaking through the Belief Barrier than others.

Additional Personal Passages

Pick out at least one passage from the Breakthrough Bible Passages above, and one of your Additional Personal Passages. Read the entire Bible chapter or section where the passages are embedded to understand their context. Explain how each speaks to your understanding of how a relationship with God suddenly appears appealing to someone, where before, they found God to be uninviting:

Breakthrough Testimony

Pray about the passages above and then write out your story of how you came to your belief and how it affects your relationship with your God now. Include the personal challenges and blessings this now provokes in your daily life and the lives of those around you:

Breakthrough Invitation

Thank You, Lord, for helping me by surrounding me with opportunities to be interact with others who have strong faith, for providing the Word to help me understand and seek out the meaning of Your desires for me. How can I not believe? Why do I fail to follow?

Adonai, in my struggle with my belief, let there be opportunity to build my faith by the inspiration of Your Spirit and the examples of others You put in my life. Let this building of faith be a testimony to those who have yet to discover You and to those who struggle in their relationship with You.

Barrier Survey

People seeking a weaker relationship with God	People seeking a stronger relationship with God

List at least one person with whom you have a relationship who appears to be seeking a weaker relationship with God (i.e. fighting for things that seem to be more selfish than selfless desires). Also list at least one person with whom you have a relationship who appears to be seeking a stronger relationship with God (i.e. fighting for things that seem to be more selfless than selfish desires). Write your observation of these people. How do they differ? How are they alike? Describe the difference you see in their unbelief and belief? How does their unbelief and belief affect their relationship with other people and with God?

THE BARRIER

The conversation in chapter 6 of *Believement* takes an interesting twist when Josh asks Adam to describe his love interest. Adam is able to go into great detail about the mannerisms, physical appearance and common interests his *special someone* possesses.

Most of us can list off the things that make any deep relationship desirable to us, or what makes one seem poisonous to us. Then looking back, after getting involved, we see that some of the attractions we experienced were actually the stuff of TV soap operas or worse yet, Wrestling Mania! Could it also be that the potential relationships we cast aside—because they seemed unworthy or unattractive—might have been the best ones for us had we delved a little deeper, pursued them more diligently?

I know, in my case, my relationship with God took a long time to develop because I didn't think it would be a good match. First, I thought God was just too boring a date—too stuffy, and frankly, I wasn't impressed.o

with the people He hung around with. Second, I was just not willing to put the time into developing a relationship that would require such attention—yes, God is a high-maintenance partner requiring lots of focus and attention!

But then, looking more closely, I recognized that God was anything but mundane and uninspiring, and that going out with Him—anywhere—was (and still is) an unpredictable and richly rewarding experience. What would have happened, I wonder, if I had missed out by saying "No thanks, You're not my type" to God?

Using a dating metaphor may seem a little too simple to describe approaching a union with the Eternal, but simplicity is where the unbeliever starts their journey. Either they simply don't want to take the time to confront and cross over the barrier separating them from the most incredible relationship they'll ever experience, or they simply aren't ready, aren't prepared, aren't inspired.

Interestingly, we often forget that God is an active suitor also. He pursues people aggressively and passionately. We may not always see it, but the thought that the Creator of the universe makes and takes that much time to court one, any person who is willing to dance with Him, should be the most incredible compliment of all. Still God can shout at you, He can move mountains, He can destroy and recreate anything that exists to prepare the table of spiritual romance, but none of that matters until someone says, "I'm listening. I want to understand. I want to meet You."

The big date can be an intimidating prospect. Sometimes we need help crossing the date barrier— sometimes we need to be introduced by a friend or by someone we see who seems radically changed by the experience. The question is, if someone was entertaining the idea of dating God, how would you introduce them?

Prayer

Creator, why do some ask, "Is there a god?" while others ask, "Who is God?" Why are we not all asking, "God, what have You made me to be?" Is this the ultimate diversionary tactic of the enemy—to distract us with concern about defining You? Why is it so difficult for me to admit that You are perfectly defined and it is me who is out of focus?

I know that Your desire to love me is why You created me. I did not create our love for one another, You did, and now that I've experienced that love, it has become impossible for me to imagine living without that love.

Because of that, I'm probably not the best person to explain to an unbeliever yet to break through the barrier, how such a love relationship with You will change them. How can I explain to those who have never tasted ice cream just how incredible the experience is? Yes, Eternal, You are so much more than ice cream, but I know You understand my point. Lord, if I am to be Your witness to those on the far side of the barrier, let my life example be a spiritual magnet to help draw them closer. Give me wisdom to share how You changed me so that they will come to desire the one I desire and step cross over to meet You spirit to Spirit.

Perspective Comparison

We all have an idea of what a great date entails—some believe they need to start with a fact-finding mission while others envision the perfect romance to reveal itself at first glance. God too wants a great first date and looks for signals. He seeks some indication, even to some microscopic degree, that we are willing to love Him, submit to Him, depend and hope in Him, serve Him, and praise Him. We can never return to Him anywhere near the love He lavishes on us, and even though He longs for anything of the list, my belief in Him (no matter how weak) and His grace to me is sufficient.

Compare and discuss the perspectives listed on both sides of Perspective Chart VI. Add additional comparisons that you believe distinguish the believer who has crossed over the barrier from the unbeliever who remains fixed on the other side. Consider your own perspective and honestly assess which of the listed traits describes you. Then write answers to the questions below:

Ask— "Do I love God completely, wanting every day to please and be closer to Him, trusting in Him for all my needs?"

If the answer is no, then— "What things, people and/or environment keeps me from fully loving and trusting in God? What am I doing to take these dis-

tractions from God out of my life so that I can walk more closely with Him?"

If the answer is yes, then— "How can I share my example of strong faith with those of no faith to help them in their decision to break through the *belief barrier* and to encourage those of weaker faith to more passionately chase after their relationship with God?"

Perspective Chart VI

Unbeliever's Barrier Perspective	Believer's Barrier Perspective
Mistrust— Moving away from God, denying his complete supremacy	Trusting— Moving toward and seeking God, acknowledging His complete supremacy
Perceive all religious people are: • Harsh and legalistic • Only about right or wrong • Rigid • Hypocritical • Judgmental • Not fun or interesting • Unforgiving • Arrogant • Condescending • Pious • Fantasy Focused, not living in reality	Recognize the blessings that belief in God return and so are willing to: • Confess— admit faulty thoughts/ behavior (sin) as compared with God's design for our thoughts/ behavior • Repent— strive to change/ correct faulty thoughts/ behavior seeking God's will • Receive Forgiveness— recognize God's power to give grace when we fail • Absolution— recognize God's love and desire to 'wipe the slate clean' after Confession, Repentance and Forgiveness are sought.
Don't think anyone's 'got it right'— everyone's so mixed up with cultures and history and people's selfish interests, that there's no way to agree; so why try?"	Sin is my nature. God can change that if I let Him.. (Spiritual Transformation). I have one power over God— to resist Him
Unsure or suspicious of the expectations a relationship with a god and what is required	Typically overestimate the requirements to please God in the relationship
Suspicious of a god's ability to be involved and committed to a relationship with one person.	Always trying to 'see' God in circumstances and events
Suspects that believing in a god is pointless or futile because there's not enough proof; so why even bother with the effort?	May question the amount of involvement God has with them individually, but acknowledges His active involvement in current events
Resistant to the idea that God is the better partner (always having both parties interest at heart) in the relationship.	Seeks (but doesn't always follow) Godly counsel

Barrier Building Questions	Barrier Breaking Questions
Why would a god want to bother having a personal relationship with a person?	Do you think maybe God would want that kind of love back; even though in your universe, God doesn't love or care?
Why be religious? Isn't it a lot of work that doesn't guarantee results?	What would be the attraction of choosing a relationship with God?
Isn't the belief in a god just a power play by some in society to get people to stay in line?	If you knew for a fact that God existed and wanted a relationship with you, what would stop you from pursuing the relationship?
Why does every religion think they're the only religion? What if your god actually just accepts everyone just as they are?	If you were able to get your questions answered about God's existence and what His will is for you, what would be the benefit?

Breakthrough Bible Passages

Deu 13:1-4, Deu 23:14, Deu 30:15-20, 2Ch 30:8-9, Job 28:28, Mat 6:30, Mat 8:26, Mat 10:32-35, Mat 14:31, Mat 16:8, Mat 17:20, Mat 26:75, Luk 12:28, Jas 4:7

Read the passages above; then write in additional personal passages that speak to you personally about why you think some people have more difficulty breaking through the Belief Barrier than others.

Additional Personal Passages

Pick out at least one passage from the Breakthrough Bible Passages above, and one of your Additional Personal Passages. Read the entire Bible chapter or section where the passages are embedded to understand their context. Explain how each speaks to your understanding of how a relationship with God suddenly appears appealing to someone, where before, they found God to be uninviting

Breakthrough Testimony

Pray about the passages above and then write out your story of any obstacles and trials that kept you from readily accepting Christ, any people who were involved in helping you recognize God's desire to love you, and any special moments when you first sensed God's presence being near to you. Describe how those moments differed from when God seemed far away or nonexistent:

Breakthrough Invitation

Master, I love Your presence in my life. What a change You have made in me by dwelling with me. I long for more of Your companionship and direction, Your love and instruction. But, Lord, there are those who can't seem to let go of their desire for control of their circumstances. I don't know if they fear or are repulsed by You, or if they simply don't care enough to step through the barrier. I can only offer my own story—the emptiness I denied before knowing you and the joy the filled me after—as testimony and as an invitation for them to ask You into their lives.

Lord, give me the strength and courage to do just that. Let my message be compelling and enticing, not for entertainment sake, but so that they can know what great things You can do with such a small life as mine. Let my example resonate with them, inviting them ever closer to a crossing over the *belief barrier*.

Barrier Survey

Sacrifices that you made to follow Christ	Benefits from your life following Christ

On the left side, describe the thing you needed to give up or relinquish- your sacrifices- to follow Christ. On the right, list the benefits you've realized since accepting Christ. In the space below, be as honest as possible and explain any of your past lifestyle- behaviors, thoughts, relationships, activities that you may either still have problems letting go of, or that you sometimes find you miss being involved in. Consider how these same types of things may hinder an unbeliever from breaking through the Belief Barrier because of their own reluctance to cast them out of their lives. How would you explain to an unbeliever your own struggle in these areas and why you made the difficult choice to try to break away from your past:

BELIEVEMENT

So it's not just about belief in God, but living out that belief, focusing only on the wants and desires of Him? That would suggest that I understand His wants and desires. That would take my studying and practicing and making mistakes, sharing those ideas with others who are doing the same thing to seek a better understanding, trying and retrying to get it right. That's a lot of work I'm talking about, It could take years!

It could take a lifetime, I hope.

I don't know about the rest of you, but when I committed my life to Christ, I was hoping for some magic pill that would *fix* my life, so that it would be exciting and beautiful all the time. I looked forward to God just being there with me whenever I wanted Him to be.

And God is here for me, just not as the Almighty Short Order Cook to satisfy my selfish appetite. The irony is that when I first came to the alter, I also misperceived my role in the relationship, thinking that, from that moment on, I had to perform at the highest possible level in any given task to gain and maintain God's love.

Grace exists for a purpose, and so does the desire God placed in me to want to please Him. But I am not created to be a participant in some kind of spiritual ability contest to prove my worthiness to the Most Worthy.

I am here to want God—nothing else. If I succeed in my earthly career, become famous (or notorious), if I struggle clumsily or glide smoothly through life, I am to love God every step of the way. As Josh explains in *Believement,* **"It's not what I have to do. It's how I live because of what's been done for me—God actually taking away my faults. My belief, combined with a commitment to actually be a legitimate example of that belief, is what God is looking for."**

My *believement.*

Love God as I live life? Sound so easy, doesn't it? Why doesn't it happen all the time then? Why do I sometimes, often, try to hide my actions or pretend that God is not right here with me. Could it be equally easy to pretend I'm alone in the universe at any chosen moment (of indiscretion) because He's not physically visible to me? Could that also be the not so secret intent of unbelievers who advocate that God does not exist—so that they can do their thing free of any outside obligation?

Believement—my living in a way that proves out my belief is not easy and is not meant to be easy. Odd isn't it that I can fall in love with someone, and they never recognize it, no matter how much I love them. Until they love me back, I am invisible, or at least inconsequential to them. God's love for me is no different, requiring only one thing to become a beautifully shared gift—I must love back.

Believement is no more and no less than the act of that offering that love, not by obligation or law, not by requirement or institution, but by surrender of my will to the will of God. That surrender is a lifelong process. I'm inconsistent in my love, but God is consistent enough in His for the both of us. That is the amazing thing about believement. It's not just my life spent learning more each day how to share love with God. It's as much (or *more!*) His eternity spent, lavishing His love on me, no matter how well I love Him back.

And if that's not enough to make things interesting, then throw into the mix some additional flavoring. Not only is my lifestyle and interrelationship with God in play, but that of all the others He counts as His posses- sion—those who have come to believe and those who will. God does want a personal relationship with each of His people, but He in no way intends for it to be private affair!

In other words, *Believement* is the walk of life that I, and my God and all His followers make together. We not only need to learn to believe alike. We need discover how to believe together!

Prayer

There came a time in my life when I reached awareness—the undeniable recognition that, You are not some distant observer who checks in on me once in a while, but a constant companion. More than that, You have demonstrated, Lord, You can be in many places at once. Behind me, nudging me on with a gentle, or not so gentle, hand of encouragement. You're beside me in all experiences, to lean on for comfort and counsel. And You're in front of me on the journey, pointing the way, waiting expectantly, challenging me to chase after You. What ignited the drive in me to begin the pursuit of You, so that now I've found that chase to have become the only desirable lifestyle for me? Something, someone beyond my faith, some spark from beyond my small- minded universe devised a way for me to discover, and a subconscious yearning to make that discovery of, You as God.

Of course I now know the answer. It was You being hyperaware that I am a distractible being, not prone to focusing and pulling together all the complexities that make up Your creation. It was You who spoke all of it, including me, into existence and when doing so, calculating not only a method for me to be salvaged from my nature to rebel against you but also constructing a means and time for me to grow and mature into something I never considered possible, an eternal child and welcomed family member into the kingdom of God.

You didn't plan it to happen in one flash of lightning. You didn't build it to be a one-time event. My choice to believe in You and in Your plan was only a starting point originating beyond the leap over the *belief barrier*. Once over the chasm, You began my *believement* adventure Lord and I praise You for the wisdom of Your way.

If the walk had been simple, the path level, the challenges uninteresting, I would have become complacent and uninspired. I might have treated You as an afterthought, a distant relative…Okay, I confess, Lord. Sometimes You did straighten the road and lighten my load along the way, and I did at times take You for granted. I'm sorry, and as much as I want to claim it won't happen again, I can't.

But that's what my *believement* is all about, isn't it, Father? If I just claim something but don't act it out, I don't really believe it.

So You have been, are, and will be helping me. Sometimes... often reacting differently from the way I want You to act on my behalf— for my needs and interests, because You know my potential better than I know myself. My refining into the best and purest of treasures for You is done in this way. I believe, but I do not always obey. I profess, but I don't always witness. I serve, but I don't always follow through. *Believement* takes practice, more for some like me than for others. And You're there, not just in the moment, but for all of my *believement*—helping me shed a skin I can't seem to shake off on my own. You provide an opportunity that I can't, that none of us who struggle with our belief and unbelief, can provide for ourselves: the chance to practice our perfection. We can't get it right without You, but with You, nothing is impossible, Lord. Thank You for being the breath, the spirit of my *believement*.

Perspective Comparison

Review again the *Biblical Statement of Faith*—either the one you revised based on your belief or the one listed in the introduction. Discuss and compare it with other believers, this time along with the perspectives listed on both sides of Perspective Chart VII. Consider your own perspective and honestly assess which of the listed traits describes your current *believement lifestyle*. Try presenting your Statement of Faith to at least one person you know who struggles with belief in God. Then write answers to the questions below:

Ask— "Before I stepped over the *belief barrier* and accepted Jesus as Savior, were there specific issues, behaviors, desires, or other beliefs I refused to let go of. If so, what were they? Do I still hold on to, or at times go back to them?"

If the answer is no, then— "What would I add and what do I not agree with. What specific Bible references do I use to justify my position of faith?"

If the answer is yes, then- "How can I overcome distractions in order to commit to a relationship with God? Do my old beliefs still surface to distract me now and do new distractions continue to tempt me? How can I share with unbelievers what my relationship with God does to help me overcome distractions? How does this impact my life, and how does it affect discussions I enter into with those who believe differently?"

Unbeliever's Barrier Perspective	Believer's Barrier Perspective
Thinks a decision to believe in a god is too complex because of the different belief systems available to choose from	Has a firm conviction that their relationship with God is right and o that their life has been radically changed because of it.
Does not think they have (or does not want to take) the time to deeply explore belief in a god and what it really entails	Sees their Believement as a desirable lifestyle, taking time, practicing, living it and breathing it, acting it out.
Thinks spiritual truth is a false hope without substance.	Has an 'Eyes Open' attitude made confident by the discovery and e embracing of spiritual truth
Unwilling to continuously examine spiritual truth in search of a full understanding	Has an internal sense of joy, peace, understanding, willingness, hope and perfect love that is difficult s, to articulate, but that influences all their actions, conversations, behaviors and thoughts.
Distracted by seeking satisfaction in emotional ideals (fear, happiness, lust, hate, etc.) instead of seeking spiritual completion (joy, peace, understanding, willingness, hope, perfect love).	Wants to seek God as the 'first purpose' in life, waking up wanting, to know more about Him, asking for Him to guide and instruct and to reveal His will for the individual. Goes to bed at night wanting to be more like Jesus the next day
Lack a foundation of deeper study, thinking their beliefs must remain 'flexible' or 'changeable'	
Treat belief casually, not fully testing and investigating spiritual truth	Possesses a rational approach to faith founded on prayer and studied spiritual truth resulting in a lifestyle that looks 'unbelievable' to unbelievers

Barrier Building Questions	Barrier Breaking Questions
What is it about Christians and other religious types that make them think their gods are cou so special?	Tell me about your beliefs. What do you believe so strongly that you couldn't live without those beliefs?
Isn't there a way we can all just live stro and let live- allowing people to believe whatever they want to?	Why can't you live without your strong beliefs?
If the lifestyle I've chosen doesn't mesh with yours, does that mean Ass I'm not good enough for you? Does that mean I have to change to make you happy?	Are you willing to examine the flaws we all share as humans?
Even if there is a god, what is happening in the world today that flaw shows he cares about whether or not we believe in him. If he exists, pers won't he exist whether or not I believe in him?	Assuming you agree that we as humans have common flaws which have damaged humankind on a large scale: If there was one perfect person who actually had no flaws, who was willing to help take the flaws of others away if they would believe in and follow the perfect person as God; would you worship and follow that person?

Breakthrough Bible Passages

Neh 1:5-10, Psa 34:11-22, Psa 37:27-40, Pro 4:13-27, Pro 30:8-9, Jer 26:13-15, Eze 20:14-26, Mat 26:34-35, Luk 17:1-10, 1Th 1:11-12, 2Ti 2:10-15, 1Pe 3:8-17

Read the passages above; then write in additional personal passages that speak to you personally about Your Believement- the lifestyle you lead that continues to bring you closer to God.

Additional Personal Passages

Pick out at least one passage from the Breakthrough Bible Passages above, and one of your Additional Personal Passages. Read the entire Bible chapter or section where the passages are embedded to understand their context. Explain how each speaks to your understanding of how you are to live for God. What are your expectations of the relationship and what is His? How is your Believement different than the lifestyle of an unbeliever's? How does that affect your daily living? Describe how or if your Believement is an effective witness to the world:

Breakthrough Testimony

Pray about the passages above and then write out your story of what your lifestyle, attitudes, and beliefs were before accepting Jesus Christ as your Lord and Savior. Then describe your walk daily with God now, what this changed lifestyle—your *believement*—has done to your life and how you see it affecting your future.

Breakthrough Invitation

I now know beyond a shadow of any doubt, Lord, that You exist. I know, without question, that I am Your child and that You love me despite my failed attempts at loving You. I know, Master, that there was (and is) a larger plan than I, or any person, could conceive, that You were, and are, the architect of that plan. I understand that the plan involves an eternity in which someway, I'm involved. I know all I have to do is to admit I'm incapable of correcting my faults on my own, ask for Your love, strive to love You as You love me^ *mean* all of this in the deepest part of me instead of just speaking the words…and. I'll be part of that eternal paradise.

Master, I realize that just saying these things is not enough. I believe them with all my heart. I know the belief of these things has changed who I am inwardly and what I do outwardly. Lord, I ask that those I encounter who are unbelievers either by conviction or lifestyle are challenged by my *believement*. I pray that Your work in me and through me invites them closer to breaking through the *belief barrier* and moving further beyond the barrier into their own life of *believement* with You.

Barrier Survey

Lifestyle after accepting Jesus	Lifestyle before accepting Jesus

On the left side in the box above, before accepting Jesus, describe what your life looked like- how did your unbe- lievement affect you, your family, your friends and associates, your job, your community, etc? On the right side in the box above, after accepting Jesus, describe what your life now looks like- how does your Believement affect you, your family, your friends and associates, your job, your community, etc?

Below, detail how you would explain to an unbeliever who is not committed to Christ, the distinctions of how your life impacted the world before accepting Christ vs. the impact God is allowing you to make now:

LIVING TRUTH

"Jesus Christ is **my Savior and Lord, but like I said, I'm not asking you to believe anything. I just told you what I believe. I had big problems with it too; then realized there was no other way for God to fix my flaws so that we could have the relationship we do. I don't expect you to understand. Like I said: The great and powerful message is really…**"

"Yeah, yeah, I got it, '**is really a small and very personal message,**' and you're not the one to best explain it. But you still haven't answered my question. Who can explain it?"

Josh and Adam conversing in chapter 7 of
Believement: Breaking Through the Belief Barrier

Josh's testimony in chapter 7 about how God reached out to him in his early life is actually borrowed from my own walk to the altar. Who knew then how much the internal workings of a rebellious and espoused atheist would be retooled just from joining that group. Yet it was just a beginning.

There were many people in my life that helped shape and steer the choice I made to believe in and follow my Lord. Some were more influential than others; some had small roles with huge results. I'm grateful to each, and as I look back, I realize that behind the scene, the Spirit of God was influencing them and me. It's still difficult for me to realize that I was a personal pet project of God's. I think that concept—a perfect God willing working to individually relate with a flawed individual person—is the biggest hurdle of all for an unbeliever to overcome. It was for me.

But I have the benefit of 20/20 hindsight. I look back in total and wonder at what I now coin as *the miracles behind*—all the events, circumstances, relationships, and outcomes that directed my life on a much different, amazingly wonderful path. A path I would never have dreamed possible or doable on my own.

That's my past. Believement is all about what happens from this point forward—from the breaking through of the barrier and far beyond. It's not a moment in time or even the culmination of time. *Believement* is nothing more than trusting in and living out *the miracles ahead*—all the events, circumstances, relationships, and outcomes that God has already planned for in our lives. The closer our *believement* path resembles His *believement* path, the more amazing the journey.

So how to describe this adventure to someone watching from the outside—how do I convince someone that God exists, that everything the Bible says is true? How do I explain that suspicious spiritual encounters may indeed be legitimate efforts at cross-barrier communication from forces unseen and unknown? It can't be done. Does that mean I shouldn't, we shouldn't, be involved in the events leading up to an unbeliever's ultimate spiritual encounter?

When all the rhetoric is spouted, when all the posturing and explaining and imploring of one person to another to adapt new beliefs is done, one thing remains evident; the decision to believe in God and follow Jesus Christ as Lord and Savior is not a group event. It's not a Sunday morning altar call or a sinners' prayer led by someone else on your behalf. It is the deepest of personal conversations with the unfathomable God of the universe. One on one, no others involved—confession, repentance, invitation, acceptance— one person, one God, one choice. The altar at which this rendezvous takes place can either be a seemingly insurmountable barrier, or it can be the passage to a dwelling place of untold beauty and joy.

But as the story tells, there is preparation to be done, and God is notorious for using His greatest tools to make the ground ready. Those tools are people, those who influence and shape our lives, good or bad, toward making the biggest of choices.

What we all face at the altar is one simple thing: truth. Some would argue that there are different kinds of truth—it's their way of avoiding the most basic questions on the most elemental truths.

Is there, or is there not, a God?

Truth meets us right where we are, sometimes slapping us down hard, other times just invisibly challenging us to seek it out. At some point, though, it refuses to be ignored or postponed. Truth does not go away. It is a living thing, a presence that I cannot kill or destroy no matter how much I pretend it doesn't exist.

Living truth is hard to explain to someone not living in truth, and frankly, I'm not the one who can best explain it. But if I'm not, who can?

The answer is one of the simplest and most complex truths of all.

With God's help, you can.

Prayer

There was a time in a place, not too awful long ago, when I don't believe I believed in You as a real, tangible, touchable entity, Lord. There was a time and place where You became a target of my distain, something to intellectually disprove and dismiss as a novelty. To me, You were a weakness of self-confidence in those who sought after and worshiped You.

I say I don't believe I believed in You then, but actually I don't know if I actually didn't believe, or if I was just fighting my beliefs. Was I just struggling to be an individual who stood out apart from the mind-numbed pack—those who all seemed to be thinking and believing the same thing?

Master, I wonder who else is out there are still fighting and whether they are in the same place I had been? If someone chooses to live in that place, does that place become so familiar to them that they build their home, their whole philosophy and theology and way of living—their *believement*—based on that location?

And going off the deep end, as long as I'm making up words, I might as well charge ahead boldly—I think all of humankind develops a *believement* to support their preferred beliefs. That's why I see people

firmly planting their feet on a position that sounds astoundingly absurd to me, yet to them, it seems perfectly righteous. I'm sure they think the same way of me, Jehovah. So why is my believement better than their believement?

But there is an answer, isn't there, Lord? It doesn't come from my believement, but from *Your* believement, because before I could believe, You believed in me. Before I had the ability to believe, You invented the idea of belief and spoke it into existence. You gave everyone's belief and *believement* the freedom to exist. Your incredible love even allowed for the freedom of all people in your creation— whose love You still desperately desire—to choose a *believement* that does not include Your existence. Tragically sad, but beautiful in that You designed our freedom to choose our own believement into Your *believement* so that our chosen love for You is genuine. I am astounded, Adonai, and I thank You for Your creation of so profound a *believement relationship*.

Perspective Comparison

Chapter 8 of *Believement: Breaking Through the Belief Barrier* is purposefully short in content but long in consideration. Several questions will come immediately to mind when reading the finale. How do we all handle mortality, conviction, opportunities for salvation? As believers, how do we react and reach out to others in those rare personal moments we share together? I'm sure you'll think of more. Before completing this study, however, consider the following corollaries with others:

Believement Relationship Corollaries

*Not all humans believe in God, but
all of us do have unbelief.*

*We share something inherently in common with
our Creator—We desire deeply committed love
from someone who believes in us deeply.*

To believers, God's love for us isn't something that needs to be proven to exist. Its existence is revealed by belief. Someone who denies the existence of God but seeks His love will only see unconnected circumstances and coincidences—chance acts, random events, natural or unnatural activity in the world—and they'll write the unexplainable off as...unexplainable.

It would be like trying to prove to someone that an apple bought in a store came off a tree when the person has never seen or heard of an apple tree. It they're unwilling to trust your explanation, they'll have trouble trusting in, or finding value in the correlation. The apple is in the store. Does it matter where it came from?

This last perspective comparison segment includes an extra step. Consider and pray about the entire idea of *believement* as a lifestyle dedicated to God as described in the book. Reread the **Believement Relationship Corollaries** and answer the following question from the perspective of believer whose faith may be challenged:

> *If I still struggle with unbelief, but there is a source of love that will help me grow more in my belief—why not pursue it, why not love God?*

Then try to examine the corollaries from the perspective of an unbeliever on the other side of the *belief barrier*:

> *I see no proof of a God who loves me. What's wrong with looking for my love—for someone who believes in me—where I can see real evidence of it?*

Discuss the relationship corollaries and the two questions above along with the perspectives listed on both sides of Perspective Chart VIII. Add additional comparisons that you believe distinguish the believer from the unbeliever. Add additional comparisons that you believe distinguish the believer from the unbe-

liever. Consider your own perspective and honestly assess which of the listed traits describes you. Then write answers to the questions below:

Ask— "At the bedside of someone who is terminally ill (but still cognizant of things happening around them), would I be able to converse with them confidently about their belief or unbelief?"

If the answer is no, then— "How should I now be preparing myself for that possibility? What would I do if someone close to me needed my witness of faith—for me to share my love of God with them—at any given moment? What would I expect of those close to me if I suddenly became terminally ill or critically wounded?"

If the answer is yes, then— "How significant is my *believement* lifestyle as a witness to those whose unbelief of God is stronger than their belief in God? Not being able to judge someone's inner convictions, how can I help others see the power and love of God in a way that helps draw them closer to Him, no matter where they are on the line between believement and unbelievement?"

Unbeliever's Barrier Perspective	Believer's Barrier Perspective
Unwilling to commit fully to believing in a god—reluctant to dedicate focus and change lifestyle—skeptical of godly characteristics: His including the willingness to love someone enough to 'self-sacrifice' for a mutually perfect relationship	Committed to believing in God— dedicating focus and life to Him— willing to recognize His characteristics: including His willingness to love someone enough to sacrifice Himself so that they can have a perfect relationship.
Is suspicious of the concept of a change' whereby someone becomes a totally different person spiritually.	Trusting of the concept of a spiritual change' whereby someone becomes a totally different person spiritually
Sees prayer as a quaint tradition or as 'self talk, not necessarily directed in conversation to a god	Sees prayer as a two way conversation on a spiritual level with God
May read or hear about what a By god desires, but views most or all abo documentation as strictly 'human' inspired.	By reading and hearing and praying about what God desires, becomes increasingly attracted to the lifestyle those desires implied.
Judgmental of people who claim to have accurately defined their god and who insist their definition to be exclusively accurate and true	Understanding that the very nature of human free will requires each individual to make their own choice of belief
Finds it difficult to recognize and Rec accept the benefits of abandoning of a personal choice in favor of a god's fav will in all things	Recognizes and accepts the benefits of abandoning personal choice in favor of God's will in all things
Defines life and death physically with an afterlife being an unknown factor that is not worth prolonged consideration under normal circumstances	Defines life and death spiritually instead of physically; life being a total and eternal relationship with God; and death being a total and eternal absence of the presence of God

Barrier Building Questions	Barrier Breaking Questions
Don't I get a say in what I want? Didn't your god make this world to be enjoyed and used?	What do you want to do? What's the most important thing you want to be appreciated and remembered for?
If living this godly life of yours is so great, why are Christian and other religious people's lives so messed up?	When your life is really messed up and you can't find solutions or remedies, who do you go to for help?
Weren't some of the great atrocities in world history done by Christians?	Does my being flawed prevent a perfect and all powerful God from offering forgiveness to me and finding a way to 'fix' me?
What's the rush? Can't I live the life I want and get serious about deciding if I believe in a god when I get old and have nothing else to do?	Tell me the date your life will end? What if your decision to not follow God changes the outcome of your future forever? What if you're wrong?

Breakthrough Bible Passages

Psa 91:11-12, Psa 22:9-11, Psa 139:13-16, Pro 13:17-25, Isa 25-1-12, 2, Jer 29:11-13, Jer 32:37-42, Luk 15:1-10, Luk 17:20-36, Joh 13:37-38, Joh 15:26-27, 1Cor 3:3-13, Rev 3:15-20

Read the passages above; then write in additional personal passages that speak to you personally about the truth of God's existence, His love for you personally and the plans He has for you.

Additional Personal Passages

Pick out at least one passage from the Breakthrough Bible Passages above, and one of your Additional Personal Passages. Read the entire Bible chapter or section where the passages are embedded to understand their context. Explain how each speaks to your understanding of the necessity of seeking the truth about God. Consider that, if He has such wonderful and eternal plans for you, does He also have the same kinds of plans, yet to be realized for unbelievers? How does your *Believement* Lifestyle and your bearing witnessing to His love factor into God's plan for the salvation of those yet to believe?

Breakthrough Testimony

Pray about the passages above and then write out your story of how God used the example of other believers in your life to help lead you to the point of making the choice to break through the *belief barrier*. Describe those believers. Were they strong believers? Was unbelief evident in their lives? How did they help you overcome your unbelief? Are these believers still active in your life? Have you thanked them for their contribution to your *believement*?

Think of at least one person you know who has not yet chosen to break through the belief barrier. Pray about whether God may be using your *believe- ment* example to bring them closer to that choice. Does the example others gave in witnessing to you help in this case?

Breakthrough Invitation

God in heaven, I'm not an expert on eternal life, but I do believe in You and in Your promise that I will be a resident in Your kingdom for eternity. I long to be at the foot of Your throne, but I know that this life You have given me now is for a purpose. I want to live according to that purpose—*Your* purpose.

Lord, I know there are those for whom the words above have little or no meaning. But the truth of the words are inescapable—to not believe in and follow You is to die spiritually. It seems such an invisible death—so inconsequential, even meaningless to this

physical world. But, Savior, it's not at all meaningless, is it? In fact You have shown this truth to be the most meaningful of all. I knew, even before I chose You as Lord, that I was dead inside. I knew something was lost, but it just didn't make sense. I thought surely I could fix it with some kind of activity or love interest or cause the world offered. I'm sorry for first choosing worldly solutions over You. Thank you for forgiving me of my first choice.

Thank You now, Adonai, for helping me, whispering to me, showing me that nothing this place has to offer could or can fix me. Thank You for helping me see the *belief barrier* clearly and offering me the choice to break through it. Thank You for saving me, for living, dying, and being resurrected for me, for personally loving me that much.

But, God of the universe, there are others who are still on the other side of the barrier. They may read this and smirk in cynicism or hunger for something past their fear and pain. I don't know. I only know that when I was where they are now, physical life seemed such a big thing filled with little hope. Help me, Master, to share the great fullness of hope, the incredible love You have given me, with them. Help them to see and choose a life beyond the physical, about the eternal, focused on one thing and one thing only—the joy of *believement* in You. Amen.

Barrier Survey

Unlike Jesus	Like Jesus

Even those who don't believe in God seem to have an opinion of the characteristics of Jesus. And, throughout the New Testament believers are instructed that our destiny is to become more and more "Christ-like' every day of our walk with Him.

On the left side in the box above, describe what you believe to be 'Not Christ-like attributes'. Next to each attribute, place an N if you do Not think you demonstrate this attribute at all; an I if you demonstrate the attribute Infrequently and an R if you regularly demonstrate the attribute. On the right side of the box, describe what you believe to be 'Christ-like attributes'. Next to each attribute, place an N if you do Not think you demonstrate the attribute at all; an I if you demonstrate the attribute Infrequently and an R if you Regularly demonstrate the attribute.

Do you have less, equal or more Rs beside Christ-like attributes than Rs beside Not Christ-like attributes? Does this suggest your belief and unbelief affect your Believement? How would an unbeliever benefit from hearing about how God has helped you with your struggles and triumphs in this area?

BIOGRAPHY

Mark Cornelius graduated from the University of North Texas with a double major in psychology and vocational rehabilitation. His background includes a successful career as an executive recruiter, business development consultant, and wealth management specialist in Nashville, Tennessee. Mark's other inter-ests involve his family and writing. Penning of other books include the following: *The Ruach Saga* including *The Singularity, The Book of Seconds and Bronzemen.*

Mark has written RUT Management: Discovering Adventure in the Routine of Life, Believement, Welfare Christianity and *Thunder Buffalo.* Mark has also penned numerous musical/video productions and maintains a popular journal ministry. Mark's talent is in finding ways to explore and present the obvious in not so obvious ways.

www.MarkCornelius.me
www.RUTManagement.com

www.ingramcontent.com/pod-product-compliance
Lightning Source LLC
Chambersburg PA
CBHW071148120626
46546CB00006B/2175